Gill Valentine
Editor

From Nowhere to Everywhere: Lesbian Geographies

From Nowhere to Everywhere: Lesbian Geographies has been co-published simultaneously as *Journal of Lesbian Studies,* Volume 4, Number 1 2000.

Pre-publication
REVIEWS,
COMMENTARIES,
EVALUATIONS . . .

"**O**ver a decade ago Gill Valentine, practically single-handedly, pioneered the study of lesbian geographies. One of the fruits of her labour is this fascinating volume that introduces the voices of a number of new lesbian geographers as well as established lesbian scholars. Focusing on spaces in Western societies–specifically, England, Canada and the United States–and at a variety of spatial scales, including virtual spaces, these studies encompass the construction of sexualities and experiences of lesbianism in both urban and rural places. This collection should be of interest to all students of social science particularly those with an interest in issues of sexualities, lesbianism and the social construction of space."

Linda Peake, PhD
Associate Professor
Division of Social Science
and Graduate Programme in Geography
York University
Toronto, Canada

From Nowhere to Everywhere: Lesbian Geographies

From Nowhere to Everywhere: Lesbian Geographies has been co-published simultaneously as *Journal of Lesbian Studies,* Volume 4, Number 1 2000.

The *Journal of Lesbian Studies* Monographic "Separates"

Below is a list of "separates," which in serials librarianship means a special issue simultaneously published as a special journal issue or double-issue *and* as a "separate" hardbound monograph. (This is a format which we also call a "DocuSerial.")

"Separates" are published because specialized libraries or professionals may wish to purchase a specific thematic issue by itself in a format which can be separately cataloged and shelved, as opposed to purchasing the journal on an on-going basis. Faculty members may also more easily consider a "separate" for classroom adoption.

"Separates" are carefully classified separately with the major book jobbers so that the journal tie-in can be noted on new book order slips to avoid duplicate purchasing.

You may wish to visit Haworth's website at . . .

http://www.haworthpressinc.com

. . . to search our online catalog for complete tables of contents of these separates and related publications.

You may also call 1-800-HAWORTH (outside US/Canada: 607-722-5857), or Fax 1-800-895-0582 (outside US/Canada: 607-771-0012), or e-mail at:

getinfo@haworthpressinc.com

From Nowhere to Everywhere: Lesbian Geographies, edited by Gill Valentine, PhD (Vol. 4, No. 1, 2000). *"A significant and worthy contribution to the ever-growing literature on sexuality and space. . . . A politically significant volume representing the first major collection on lesbian geographies. . . . I will make extensive use of this book in my courses on social and cultural geography and sexuality and space." (Jon Binnie, PhD, Lecturer in Human Geography, Liverpool, John Moores University, United Kingdom)*

Lesbians, Levis and Lipstick: The Meaning of Beauty in Our Lives, edited by Jeanine C. Cogan, PhD, and Joanie M. Erickson (Vol. 3, No. 4, 1999). *Explores lesbian beauty norms and the effects these norms have on lesbian women.*

Lesbian Sex Scandals: Sexual Practices, Indentities, and Politics, edited by Dawn Atkins, MA (Vol. 3, No. 3, 1999). *"Grounded in material practices, this collection explores confrontation and coincidence among identity politics, 'scandalous' sexual practices, and queer theory and feminism. . . . It expands notions of lesbian identification and lesbian community." (Maria Pramaggiore, PhD, Assistant Professor, Film Studies, North Carolina State University, Raleigh)*

The Lesbian Polyamory Reader: Open Relationships, Non-Monogamy, and Casual Sex, edited by Marcia Munson and Judith P. Stelboum, PhD (Vol. 3, No. 1/2, 1999). *"Offers reasonable, logical, and persuasive explanations for a style of life I had not seriously considered before. . . . A terrific read." (Beverly Todd, Acquisitions Librarian, Estes Park Public Library, Estes Park, Colorado)*

Living "Difference": Lesbian Perspectives on Work and Family Life, edited by Gillian A. Dunne, PhD (Vol. 2, No. 4, 1998). *"A fascinating, groundbreaking collection. . . . Students and professionals in psychiatry, psychology, sociology, and anthropology will find this work extremely useful and thought provoking." (Nanette K. Gartrell, MD, Associate Clinical Professor of Psychiatry, University of California at San Francisco Medical School)*

Acts of Passion: Sexuality, Gender, and Performance, edited by Nina Rapi, MA, and Maya Chowdhry, MA (Vol. 2, No. 2/3, 1998). *"This significant and impressive publication draws together a diversity of positions, practices, and polemics in relation to postmodern lesbian performance and puts them firmly on the contemporary cultural map." (Lois Keidan, Director of Live Arts, Institute of Contemporary Arts, London, United Kingdom)*

Gateways to Improving Lesbian Health and Health Care: Opening Doors, edited by Christy M. Ponticelli, PhD (Vol. 2, No. 1, 1997). *"An unprecedented collection that goes to the source for powerful and poignant information on the state of lesbian health care." (Jocelyn C. White, MD, Assistant Professor of Medicine, Oregon Health Sciences University; Faculty, Portland Program in General Internal Medicine, Legacy Portland Hospitals, Portland, Oregon)*

Classics in Lesbian Studies, edited by Esther Rothblum, PhD (Vol. 1, No. 1, 1996). *"Brings together a collection of powerful chapters that cross disciplines and offer a broad vision of lesbian lives across race, age, and community." (Michele J. Eliason, PhD, Associate Professor, College of Nursing, The University of Iowa)*

From Nowhere to Everywhere:
Lesbian Geographies

Gill Valentine
Editor

From Nowhere to Everywhere: Lesbian Geographies has been co-published simultaneously as *Journal of Lesbian Studies,* Volume 4, Number 1 2000.

Harrington Park Press
An Imprint of
The Haworth Press, Inc.
New York • London • Oxford

Published by

Harrington Park Press®, 10 Alice Street, Binghamton, NY 13904-1580 USA

Harrington Park Press® is an imprint of The Haworth Press, Inc., 10 Alice Street, Binghamton, NY 13904-1580 USA.

From Nowhere to Everywhere: Lesbian Geographies has been co-published simultaneously as *Journal of Lesbian Studies,* Volume 4, Number 1 2000.

The development, preparation, and publication of this work has been undertaken with great care. However, the publisher, employees, editors, and agents of The Haworth Press and all imprints of The Haworth Press, Inc., including The Haworth Medical Press® and Pharmaceutical Products Press®, are not responsible for any errors contained herein or for consequences that may ensue from use of materials or information contained in this work. Opinions expressed by the author(s) are not necessarily those of The Haworth Press, Inc.

Cover design by Monica Seifert.

Library of Congress Cataloging-in-Publication Data

From nowhere to everywhere : lesbian geographies / Gill Valentine, editor.
     p. cm.
     "Has been co-published simultaneously as Journal of lesbian studies, Volume 4, Number 1 2000."
     Includes bibliographical references and index.
     ISBN 1-56023-132-7 (cloth: alk. paper)–ISBN 1-56023-127-0 (pbk : alk. paper)
     1. Lesbians. 2. Human geography. 3. Spatial behavior. I. Valentine, Gill, 1965-
HQ75.5 .F76 2000
305.48'9664–dc21
                                                   00-022258

INDEXING & ABSTRACTING

Contributions to this publication are selectively indexed or abstracted in print, electronic, online, or CD-ROM version(s) of the reference tools and information services listed below. This list is current as of the copyright date of this publication. See the end of this section for additional notes.

- *Abstracts in Social Gerontology: Current Literature on Aging*

- *BUBL Information Service, an Internet-based Information Service for the UK higher education community*
  <URL: http://bubl.ac.uk/>

- *CNPIEC Reference Guide: Chinese National Directory of Foreign Periodicals*

- *Contemporary Women's Issues*

- *Feminist Periodicals: A Current Listing of Contents*

- *FINDEX (www.publist.com)*

- *Gay & Lesbian Abstracts*

- *GenderWatch*

- *HOMODOK/"Relevant" Bibliographic database, Documentation Centre for Gay & Lesbian Studies, University of Amsterdam (selective printed abstracts in "Homologie" and bibliographic computer databases covering cultural, historical, social and political aspects of gay & lesbian topics)*

- *Index to Periodical Articles Related to Law*

- *PAIS (Public Affairs Information Service) NYC (www.pais.org)*

- *Referativnyi Zhurnal (Abstracts Journal of the All-Russian Institute of Scientific and Technical Information)*

(continued)

- *Social Services Abstracts*
- *Sociological Abstracts (SA)*
- *Studies on Women Abstracts*
- *Women's Studies Index (indexed comprehensively)*

*Special Bibliographic Notes related to special journal issues
(separates) and indexing/abstracting:*

- indexing/abstracting services in this list will also cover material in any "separate" that is co-published simultaneously with Haworth's special thematic journal issue or DocuSerial. Indexing/abstracting usually covers material at the article/chapter level.
- monographic co-editions are intended for either non-subscribers or libraries which intend to purchase a second copy for their circulating collections.
- monographic co-editions are reported to all jobbers/wholesalers/approval plans. The source journal is listed as the "series" to assist the prevention of duplicate purchasing in the same manner utilized for books-in-series.
- to facilitate user/access services all indexing/abstracting services are encouraged to utilize the co-indexing entry note indicated at the bottom of the first page of each article/chapter/contribution.
- this is intended to assist a library user of any reference tool (whether print, electronic, online, or CD-ROM) to locate the monographic version if the library has purchased this version but not a subscription to the source journal.
- individual articles/chapters in any Haworth publication are also available through the Haworth Document Delivery Service (HDDS).

From Nowhere to Everywhere: Lesbian Geographies

CONTENTS

ABOUT THE EDITOR

Gill Valentine, PhD, is Professor of Human Geography at the University of Sheffield, where she teaches social geography and qualitative research methods. Her research interests include geographies of sexualities, food and foodscapes, and children, youth, and parenting. She is co-editor of *Mapping Desire: Geographies of Sexualities* (Routledge, 1995), and *Cool Places: Geographies of Youth Cultures* (Routledge, 1998), and co-author of *Consuming Geographies: You Are Where You Eat* (Routledge, 1997).

Introduction:
From Nowhere to Everywhere:
Lesbian Geographies

Gill Valentine

SUMMARY. This paper provides an introduction to this volume by outlining the emergence of lesbian geographies and the contribution they have made to understanding the mutual constitution of sexuality and space. It begins by tracing the development of these geographies from initial studies which aimed to map lesbian neighbourhoods to later work which has drawn on theorists such as Judith Butler, to explore the production and regulation of heterosexual space. It then goes on to situate the papers included in this volume within this literature by outlining their contents and the themes which crosscut them. *[Article copies available for a fee from The Haworth Document Delivery Service: 1-800-342-9678. E-mail address: getinfo@haworthpressinc.com <Website: http://www.haworthpressinc.com>]*

KEYWORDS. Geography, sexuality, lesbian, space

Gill Valentine is Professor of Human Geography at the University of Sheffield, where she teaches social geography and qualitative research methods. Her research interests include: geographies of sexualities; food and foodscapes; and children, youth and parenting. She is co-editor (with D. Bell) of *Mapping Desire: Geographies of Sexualities* (Routledge, 1995), co-author (with D. Bell) of *Consuming Geographies: You Are Where You Eat* (Routledge, 1997) and co-editor (with T. Skelton) of *Cool Places: Geographies of Youth Cultures* (Routledge, 1998).

Author note: I wish to thank Sarah O'Hara, Sarah Holloway, Ali Grant, David Bell and Jon Binnie for encouraging my own work on lesbian geographies and for their support during difficult times.

[Haworth co-indexing entry note]: "Introduction: From Nowhere to Everywhere: Lesbian Geographies." Valentine, Gill. Co-published simultaneously in *Journal of Lesbian Studies* (Harrington Park Press, an imprint of The Haworth Press, Inc.) Vol. 4, No. 1, 2000, pp. 1-9; and: *From Nowhere to Everywhere: Lesbian Geographies* (ed: Gill Valentine) Harrington Park Press, an imprint of The Haworth Press, Inc., 2000, pp. 1-9. Single or multiple copies of this article are available for a fee from The Haworth Document Delivery Service [1-800-342-9678, 9:00 a.m. - 5:00 p.m. (EST). E-mail address: getinfo@haworthpressinc.com].

1

In the late eighteenth century the British queen, Queen Victoria, when confronted by her ministers with a bill to out-law same sex sexual relationships, famously claimed that lesbians did not exist. As a result they were rendered invisible in subsequent legislation on homo-sexuality. A century later lesbian activists are queering the streets and shopping malls of the UK under slogans such as 'we are everywhere.' This transformation in lesbian visibility–from nowhere to every-where–is laden with geographical significance. It reflects the fact that lesbian identities and lifestyles are increasingly being publicly articu-lated in the urban and, though less commonly, in the rural landscape too; and that lesbians are more openly challenging the taken-for-granted production of everyday environments as heterosexual spaces.

Within the discipline of Geography, the late 1980s, but particularly the 1990s, has seen the emergence of an exciting new body of work devoted to exploring these geographies of desire (this work is re-viewed in Bell and Valentine 1995a, Grant 1998 and Binnie and Val-entine in press). Some of the first geographical work on lesbian and gay men's lives argued that they lead distinct lifestyles (defined to a lesser or greater extent by their sexuality and the reactions of others to that sexuality) which are articulated spatially, creating distinct lesbian and gay social, political and cultural landscapes. Much of this pioneer-ing work was about the lives of gay men, although notable exceptions included preliminary, and somewhat debatable, attempts by Barbara Weightman (1981) to map lesbian neighbourhoods in the US and Hilary Winchester and Paul White (1988) to locate lesbian neighbour-hoods within inner-city Paris.

Perhaps the most controversial study of lesbian and gay space was produced by the urban sociologist Manuel Castells (1983). Drawing on work conducted in San Francisco, he argued that lesbian and gay commercial and neighbourhood bases in both the US and Europe were dominated by gay men and institutions of gay male culture. And he used this as evidence first to claim that lesbians lacked similar territo-rially based communities because 'women are poorer than gay men and have less choice in terms of work and location' (1983: 140), and secondly to make rather essentialised claims about gender differences in the way men and women relate to space. He argued that men seek to dominate and therefore achieve spatial superiority, while he claimed that women have few territorial aspirations, attaching more impor-tance to social relationships.

Subsequently, a host of studies of lesbian neighbourhoods in North America and the UK have been produced to rupture Castells' assumptions (Adler and Brenner 1992, Rothenberg 1995, Peake 1993, Valentine 1995a). These all suggest that lesbians do create spatially concentrated communities but that these neighbourhoods are often composed of clusters of lesbian households and sometimes countercultural institutions such as alternative bookstores or co-operative stores rather than commercial bars and institutions. As a result these lesbian neighbourhoods often have a quasi-underground character which makes them less visible than the gay men's scene bars to those not in the know. Indeed, Peake (1993), Valentine (1995a) and Rothenberg (1995) all suggest that women often learn about lesbian neighbourhoods through word of mouth, a process neatly captured in the title of Rothenberg's essay: 'And she told two friends. . . .'

A lesbian presence is not only evident in the landscape of major towns and cities in North America and western Europe, gay women also live in and use the countryside (Bell and Valentine 1995b). Examples include Joan Nestle's account of lesbian cruising in the outdoors, and the UK magazine *The Dyke*, which has articles written by and for so-called hiking dykes, on everything from practical hillwalking skills and how to clean a sleeping bag to documenting lesbian rural cultures and the history of women in the country (Bell and Valentine 1995b).

The rural has often been imagined as an ideal environment for same-sex love in lesbian fiction, poetry and film. In the 1970s some lesbian feminists identified heterosexuality as the root of women's oppression and argued that the only way to overcome it was to distance themselves in space from hetero-patriarchal society and to create new women-centred ways of living. Although some women-only communities were established in urban areas (Egerton 1990), the aim of separatism was seen as most attainable in rural areas–because spatial isolation meant that it was easier for women to be self-sufficient in the countryside and because essentialist beliefs about women's closeness to 'nature' meant that the rural environment was regarded as a 'female space,' in contrast to the 'man-made' city (Faderman 1991). Several studies have documented these experiments to create lesbian feminist space through communal living on the land (Cheney 1985, Valentine 1997).

At the same time there has also been increased recognition of the way that everyday environments are commonly produced as heterosexual spaces, and attempts to assess the effects of the performance of sexual dissidents' identities in those spaces which are actively constructed as heterosexual (Bell et al. 1994, Valentine 1996a). These studies have drawn extensively on Judith Butler's notion of performativity (1990), arguing that the heterosexing of space is a perfomative act naturalised through repetition and regulation; and have tackled the heterosexing of space across a range of geographical scales. Sally Munt (1995), for example, has written about the way different cities are (hetero)sexed, comparing her own experiences of being a lesbian in Brighton, the so-called lesbian and gay capital of the South of England, with living in Nottingham, a city in the British Midlands which she describes as possessing a 'rugged masculinity.' The home (Johnston and Valentine 1995) and the workplace (Valentine 1993, Valentine 1996b) are also sites which have been exposed as spaces that are often encoded as heterosexual in which the presence of lesbian bodies is seen to cut in or disrupt the stability of these hegemonic productions of space.

Indeed, Geography itself has also been subject to the same critique by sexual dissidents who have challenged its heteronormative, ableist, masculinist and colonial heritage (Chouinard and Grant 1995, Grant 1998, Valentine in press). Observing the lack of 'out' lesbian geographers within the academy, Grant (1998) comments that: 'There is an incredible irony in the fact that as we move towards self-consciously situated, *embodied* geographies there has been an associated emergence of strangely migratory, *disembodied* queer geographies.' This invisibility is perhaps explained by Louise Johnson (1994: 110), who, writing about her own anxieties about coming out in the geographical workplace, explains that: 'I've agonised for years about the consequences–professional and otherwise–of 'coming out' in print, declaring my own sexuality and building a feminist geography upon my lesbianism. And basically, I've seen the risks as too great, the stakes as too high in a homophobic culture and discipline.'

Regulatory regimes constrain possible performances of sexual identities in order to maintain the seeming 'naturalness' of heterosexuality. These are regimes which take the form of multiple 'processes, of different origin and scattered location, regulating the most intimate and minute elements of the construction of space, time, desire and embodiment' (Foucault 1979: 138). In the UK, for example, a number of statutory and common laws can be, and often are, used to criminalise public displays of same-sex desire on the streets (Valentine 1996a), while there is mounting evidence of widespread anti-lesbian discrimination and anti-lesbian violence in 'public' and 'private' spaces (Berrill 1992). As a result it is not surprising that many lesbians manage their identities in different spaces in order to 'pass' as heterosexual (Bell and Valentine 1995b).

Of course while the hegemonic performance of many everyday spaces is usually heterosexual, that is not to say that spaces are produced in a singular or uniform way. Rather the identity of spaces, like the identities of individuals, are always cross cut with multiple contradictions and tensions. So that for example, lesbians can produce their own relational spaces or read heterosexual space against the grain, experiencing it and producing it differently. Dress, language, music are just some of the vehicles which have been used to mobilise such relational spaces (Valentine 1995b).

Probyn points out that 'Lesbian desires and manners of being can restructure space' (Probyn 1995: 81) in many different ways. Describing a hypothetical scenario of two lesbians kissing in a front of a bar full of men, Elspeth Probyn explains how they (re)produce space. She writes: "while their kiss cannot undo the historicity of the ways in which men produce their space as the site of production of gender (Woman) for another (men), the fact that a woman materialises another woman as the object of her desire does go some way in rearticulating that space. The enactment of desire here can begin to skewer the lines of force that seek to constitute women as Woman, as object of the masculine gaze . . . making out in straight space can be a turn-on, one articulation of desire that bends and queers a masculine place allowing for a momentarily sexed lesbian space" (Probyn 1995: 81).

Other examples of lesbian attempts to bend and queer space include the direct action group the Lesbian Avengers. From small beginnings–a group of five activists led by the American writer Sarah Schulman–the Lesbian Avengers have grown in numbers and strength, sometimes collaborating with other groups such as Las Buenas Amigas and African Ancestral Lesbians for Societal Change (Meono-Picado 1995). Their aim is to make lesbians visible in both heterosexual and queer spaces. Actions have included invading a major store in London and taking over its window display by labelling the mannequins 'designer Dyke,' Lesbian Boy. Lynda Johnston's work on the HERO parade, New Zealand's largest lesbian and gay pride festival, and the Sydney Mardi Gras in Australia, demonstrates the potential of lesbian and gay festivals to temporally re-code public space.

This collection of essays therefore marks a further step in the transformation in the visibility of lesbian geographies and geographers from nowhere to everywhere. Each explores a different take on 'space,' while at the same time there are many shared themes which crosscut the authors' consideration of lesbian geographies. Sarah Elwood opens this volume with a nuanced account of lesbians' experiences of home, based on research in Minneapolis and St. Paul, Minnesota, US. While as this review demonstrates, geographers have made important inroads into documenting lesbians' uses and experiences of so-called public spaces such as the neighbourhood, the community and the street; the home has remained a relatively neglected space. In her paper Elwood demonstrates that homes, as sites of identity formation and 'private' spaces where lesbians can contest dominant cultural norms and develop a lesbian culture, can represent sanctuaries or spaces of liberation for women. Yet at the same time the home can also be a 'public' or visible marker of lesbian presence in a neighbourhood. As such, the lesbian home, rather than being a private and safe space, can become a vulnerable location where lesbians encounter harassment and hostility from property owners and neighbours. In this way Elwood's paper plays an important part in contesting dichotomous geographical concepts such as 'public' and 'private.'

Homes of course are nested within neighbourhoods and in turn within communities. In the following paper Jenny Lo and Theresa Healy move up this scale to consider lesbians' experiences of 'community' in the city of Vancouver, Canada. While drawing on the insights of an established body of work on lesbian and gay neighbourhoods, Lo and Healy move away from thinking of 'community' in terms of unity and homogeneity. Rather, they recognise the multiplicity and diversity of lesbian 'communities' which exist in Vancouver, exploring the different sorts of space lesbians have created for themselves in East versus West Vancouver. Like the paper by Elwood, this paper also raises important questions about lesbian visibility and geographical concepts of 'public' and 'private.'

'Community' is also a theme touched on in Celeste Wincapaw's essay on lesbians' and bi-sexual women's use of computer-mediated communications. While Lo and Healy's paper examined the creation of lesbian space within the urban landscape, by focusing on electronic mailing lists on the Internet, Wincapaw considers lesbian and bisexual women's attempts to create 'virtual' space for themselves. Questions of the policing of identity and of harassment, themes commonly described in geographical work on lesbians' experiences of the street, are also all too apparent in her account of 'virtual space.'

In the fourth paper of this collection Ali Grant considers the threat that multiple lesbian identities pose to heterosexual hegemony across space through considering the interconnected processes which operate to regulate and contain anti-violence activism in the city of Hamilton, Canada. Drawing on the theoretical writings of Judith Butler (1990) about the role of the regulatory fictions of sex and gender in the maintenance of compulsory heterosexuality, Grant considers how aspects of political activism constitute 'UnWomanly Acts'; and how the marginalisation and punishment of lesbian activists reinforces the regulatory power of the terms 'lesbian' and 'woman,' reducing the potential of these acts. In this paper, the concept of lesbian 'visibility' is important in understanding both the radical potential of anti-violence activism and also its regulation and containment.

The issue of lesbian visibility–this time within the academy–is also evident in my own essay which follows on from Grant's. This outlines my personal experience of being harassed through hate mail and silent phone calls. Through exploring the different processes through which my harasser has sought to exclude me from the discipline of Geography my paper considers some of the complex contradictions between my 'public' identity as a lesbian within Geography and my 'private' life; and the way that such divisions between 'work' and 'home' can be breached. In doing so it thus highlights the way personal geographies can be taken for granted until they are transgressed.

The final essay by Cyndra MacDowall neatly captures many of the concepts apparent in the other papers, particularly the twin issues of visibility and invisibility, by providing a largely visual account of, among other things, the ambiguity of lesbian identity, homo/lesbian eroticism and women's access to and ownership of public space. Her images convey the sense that 'we are everywhere' while also exposing lesbian invisibility in the landscape. The sense of movement articulated in this personal narrative of travel and identity also marks the convergence of some of the geographical spaces discussed in the previous essays in this collection; and articulates a sense of 'movement' in terms of the development of lesbian space, place, memory and history. Hopefully, by focusing on the centrality of spatiality in lesbian lives yet also problematising geographical terms such as public and private, this collection of essays will mark one more step in the journey of critical geographers to chart lesbian geographies and to raise the profile of lesbian geographers.

REFERENCES

Adler, S. and Brenner, J. 1992: Gender and space: lesbians and gay men in the city: *International Journal of Urban and Regional Research* 16, 24-34.

Bell, D. and Valentine, G., editors, 1995a: *Mapping desire: geographies of sexualities*. London: Routledge.

Bell D. and Valentine, G. 1995b: Queer country: rural lesbian and gay lives. *Journal of Rural Studies* 11, 113-22.

Bell, D. and Valentine, G. 1995c: The sexed self: strategies of performance, sites of resistance. In Pile, S. and Thrift, N. editors, *Mapping the subject: geographies of cultural transformation*. London: Routledge.

Bell, D., Binnie, J., Cream, J. and Valentine, G. 1994: All hyped up and no place to go. *Gender, Place and Culture* 1, 31-47.

Berrill, K. 1992: Anti-gay violence and victimisation in the United States: an overview, in Herek, G. and Berrill K. editors, *Hate crimes: confronting violence against lesbians and gay men*: London: Sage.

Binnie, J. and Valentine, G. (in press) Geographies of sexuality: a review of progress *Progress in Human Geography*.

Butler, J. 1990: *Gender trouble: feminism and the subversion of identity*. London: Routledge.

Castells, M. 1983: *The city and the grassroots*. Berkeley, CA: University of California Press.

Cheney, J. 1985: *Lesbian Land*: Minneapolis: Word Weavers.

Chouinard, V. and Grant, A. 1995: On being not even anywhere near the project: ways of putting ourselves in the picture *Antipode* 27, 137-166.

Egerton, J. 1990: Out but not down: lesbians' experiences of housing *Feminist Review* 36, 75-88.

Faderman, L. 1991: *Odd girls and twilight lovers: A history of lesbian life in twentieth-century America*: Harmondsworth: Penguin.

Foucault, M. 1979: *Discipline and punish* New York: Vintage.

Grant, A. 1998: Dyke Geographies: all over the place. In Griffin, G. editor *Straight Studies Modified* London: Wisepress.

Johnson, L. 1994: What future for feminist geography? *Gender, Place and Culture* 1, 103-13.

Johnston, L. 1996: Embodying tourism. Proceedings of Tourism Down Under II Conference. 3-6 December, University of Otago, Dunedin, New Zealand, copy available from author, Department of Geography, Waikato University, Hamilton, New Zealand.

Johnston, L. and Valentine, G. 1995: Wherever I lay my girlfriend that's my home: the performance and surveillance of lesbian identities in domestic environments. In Bell, D. and Valentine, G., editors: *Mapping desire: geographies of sexualities.* London: Routledge.

Meono-Picado, P. 1995: Redefining the barricades: latina lesbian politics and the appropriation of public space, paper presented at the New Horizons in Feminist Geography conference, Kentucky, US. Available from the author at the School of Geography, Clark University, US.

Munt, S. 1995: The lesbian flaneur. In Bell, D. and Valentine, G., editors, *Mapping desire: geographies of sexualities*, London: Routledge, 114-25.

Peake, L. 1993: 'Race' and sexuality: challenging the patriarchal structuring of urban social space. Environment & Planning D: Society & Space 11, 415-32.

Probyn, E. 1995: Lesbians in space. gender, sex and the structure of missing *Gender, Place and Culture* 2, 1: 77-84.

Rothenberg, T. 1995: 'And she told two friends': lesbians creating urban social space. In Bell, D. and Valentine, G., editors, *Mapping desire: geographies of sexualities,* London: Routledge, 165-81.

Valentine, G. 1993: (Hetero)sexing space: lesbian perceptions and experiences of everyday spaces. *Environment and Planning D: Society and Space* 11, 394-413.

Valentine, G. 1995a: Out and about: geographies of lesbian landscapes. *International Journal of Urban and Regional Research* 19, 96-112.

Valentine, G. 1995b: Creating transgressive space: the music of kd lang *Transactions of the Institute of British Geographers* 20: 474-85.

Valentine, G. 1996a: (Re)negotiating the heterosexual street. In Duncan, N. editor: *Bodyspace* London: Routledge.

Valentine, G. 1996b: An equal place to work? Discrimination and sexual citizenship in the European Union in Garcia-Ramon, M.D. and Monk, J. editors, *Women of the European Union: the politics of work and daily life.* London: Routledge. 111-125.

Valentine, G. 1997: Making space: lesbian separatist communities in the United States in Cloke, P. and Little J., editors, *Contested Countryside Cultures.* London: Routledge.

Valentine, G., 1998: Sticks and stones may break my bones: a personal geography of harassment *Antipode.*

Weightman, B. 1981: Commentary: towards a geography of the gay community. *Journal of Cultural Geography* 1, 106-12.

Winchester, H. and White P. 1988: The location of marginalised groups in the inner city. *Environment and Planning D: Society and Space* 6, 37-54.

Lesbian Living Spaces:
Multiple Meanings of Home

Sarah A. Elwood

SUMMARY. This paper is an exploration of lesbian living spaces, focusing on the diverse experiences and meanings of home and neighborhood in lesbian communities. These issues are developed from interviews conducted with lesbians in the metropolitan area of Minneapolis and St. Paul, Minnesota. Lesbian communities are heterogeneous, made up of individuals who might share a common sexual identity, but differ in their race, class, religious, or ethnic identity. Thus, lesbian living spaces have multiple meanings for the individuals and communities who create and live in them. In so far as these spaces are sites of identity formation and spaces in which some lesbians contest dominant cultural norms, they are places of liberation. But because they are sometimes simultaneously places where lesbians encounter harassment and discrimination, they are places of oppression. I will argue that these contradictory meanings make it impossible to define these living spaces as absolutely 'public' or 'private' spaces. *[Article copies available for a fee from The Haworth Document Delivery Service: 1-800-342-9678. E-mail address: getinfo@haworthpressinc.com <Website: http://www.haworthpressinc.com>]*

KEYWORDS. Home, lesbian, community, identities

Sarah A. Elwood is a graduate student in the department of geography at the University of Minnesota in Minneapolis, Minnesota. Her research interests include feminist and social geography and GIS (Geographic Information Systems). She is currently researching the social impacts of GIS use by local community activist groups in Minneapolis.

Address correspondence to: Sarah A. Elwood, University of Minnesota, Department of Geography, 414 Social Sciences Tower, 267 19th Ave. S., Minneapolis, MN 55455 (e-mail: elwo0005@maroon.tc.umn.edu).

Author note: I am grateful to Lisa Disch, Hilda Kurtz, Helga Leitner, and anonymous reviewers for comments on previous drafts.

[Haworth co-indexing entry note]: "Lesbian Living Spaces: Multiple Meanings of Home." Elwood, Sarah A. Co-published simultaneously in *Journal of Lesbian Studies* (Harrington Park Press, an imprint of The Haworth Press, Inc.) Vol. 4, No. 1, 2000, pp. 11-27; and: *From Nowhere to Everywhere: Lesbian Geographies* (ed: Gill Valentine) Harrington Park Press, an imprint of The Haworth Press, Inc., 2000, pp. 11-27. Single or multiple copies of this article are available for a fee from The Haworth Document Delivery Service [1-800-342-9678, 9:00 a.m. - 5:00 p.m. (EST). E-mail address: getinfo@haworthpressinc.com].

> *Home represents a great deal to me–touching a woman without a*
> *trace of defiance or self-consciousness, feeling 'real' and having*
> *my life witnessed. (Egerton, 1990)*

Home is powerful idea, one which is loaded with complex expectations, memories, and experiences. In the experiences of minority cultures for whom daily life outside the home may be fraught with a wide variety of struggles, home can take on particular significance as a place of belonging. For instance, in the description above, home is the place where a lesbian is at last acknowledged and able to live her identity without being self-conscious. The literature on lesbian geographies has conceptualized the private space of the home as a place of refuge, a place where lesbians can be removed from the prying eyes of the public and be free to express their sexual identity (Valentine, 1993b; Johnston and Valentine, 1995). It is a place where lesbians can express their sexuality out of public view and gather with other lesbians (Kennedy and Davis, 1993). Within an often-hostile society, the home provides an important space within which lesbians can sometimes escape the direct antagonism they face in more public spaces.

In the geographic literature, home has been broadly conceived of as a place of privacy, shelter, and belonging (Somerville, 1992). The meaning of home in lesbian experience is more complicated than these explanations. Certainly, lesbian homes can be a place of refuge and sheltering invisibility. Existing in an environment of fairly frequent discrimination and harassment, it would be naive to argue otherwise. But for some lesbians, home is also a site where they make their sexual identity visible in a conscious attempt to challenge assumptions of heterosexuality and to contest societal pressures to confine and hide lesbian sexuality within private spaces (Rich, 1989). These homes are places in which to nurture, maintain and actively assert lesbian identity. At the same time, the lesbian home encompasses contradictory meanings. The home might be a place of affirmation, a place where a lesbian feels most comfortable expressing her sexual identity. Simultaneously, it is often a place to which such expressions are rigidly confined by societal disapproval and harassment. Some of the same contradictions exist in lesbian neighborhoods. While these areas might be places where lesbians form secure, affirming communities, they might also be places where lesbians are oppressed.

In lesbian experience, homes and neighborhoods are imbued with multiple layers of meanings for the different people and communities who inhabit these spaces. The meanings attached to lesbian living spaces vary because diverse individuals and communities experience these spaces differently. These lesbian living spaces disrupt our understanding of the differences between public and private space. In many lesbian experiences of living spaces, the private is made public. Whether these spaces are ultimately understood as public or private, they are highly politicized. Lesbian living spaces are directly involved in struggles over identity, control of social spaces, and social power.

I develop these ideas based on a set of intensive interviews conducted with lesbians in the Minneapolis/St. Paul metropolitan areas (hereafter referred to as the Twin Cities) in which they described their families, choices of homes, activities, and movements throughout the area. These women are all between 30 and 55 years old and most have lived in the Twin Cities area since the mid-1970s. Some identified as working class, others as middle class, others as upper middle class. They had different ethnic and religious backgrounds. Some chose to live in lesbian neighborhoods, others did not. Some lived in central city neighborhoods, others in the suburbs. Some lived alone, others lived with lovers, some lived with several house mates, and some lived with children. Some participated in activities of the larger Twin Cities lesbian community or patronized lesbian establishments and others did not. Along with these differences, there was one striking similarity among the participants' backgrounds that I think significantly affects their understandings of their homes and neighborhoods. All came out as lesbians during the 1970s and participated in different ways in the local lesbian feminist communities. Thus, though they belonged to different social circles, they shared common roots in a politically aware "activist" lesbian-feminist culture. I suspect that this common background contributes to their relatively high level of openness about their sexual identity and to their conscious recognition of their homes and neighborhoods as politically contested spaces.

IDENTITY AND MEANINGS OF PLACE IN LESBIAN COMMUNITIES

The geographic literature on home, family, and domestic space has raised important questions about the gendered meanings and experiences of homes and families, particularly as they affect women (Loyd,

1982; McDowell, 1983; Madigan et al., 1990). For the most part, this literature has focused implicitly on heterosexually gendered relations in space, problematizing the meanings of home along gender lines, but failing to problematize differences in these meanings that might occur based on sexuality.[1] Lesbian meanings of home contradict and complicate much of what has been written by geographers about domestic spaces. For instance, some scholars argue that the home is understood as a place of privacy, a place where occupants have the power to set boundaries beyond which other individuals might not pass (Ryan, 1983; Somerville, 1992). In contrast, I will show how for many lesbians, home is not private, but rather a place of surveillance by a dominantly heterosexual and sometimes hostile world. Most are highly aware of this surveillance, and the ways that their homes hide or reveal their sexual identity to neighbors, visitors, or straight family members with whom they share a home. The literature has also explained how the social construction of home in capitalist societies tends to maximize isolation between family units (McDowell, 1983). I will show that for some lesbian families, this is not the case–homes are created and shared in networks of mutual support that bring families together. Lesbian experiences also contradict any understandings of homes as a place of refuge and safety. I will show that safety is a complicated concept in lesbian experience and homes that in many instances are not 'safe,' but rather are places where lesbians may be targeted for harassment or forced to hide their sexual identity. These contradictions illustrate the necessity of examining the role of sexual identity in shaping the meanings of domestic spaces.

In seeking to understand lesbian living space, it is important to understand that lesbian identity is heterogeneous and experiences of home are influenced by much more than sexual identity. Rather, sexual identity is just one piece of a multi-faceted identity that shapes a lesbian's experiences and perceptions of different spaces. For instance, lesbians experience the world based on their identities both as women and as members of a sexual minority group (Adler and Brenner, 1992). As women they have less economic power than men and as a result, gender and class are often closely related in their effects. This is apparent in one woman's description of her difficult search for rental housing:

> At that time [in the Twin Cities] it was the landlord's market to choose tenants . . . and one of my difficulties was that I was a

single woman who was unemployed. And no one wanted to rent to me.

Another woman described similar problems finding housing because she was alternately self-employed, or working inconsistently at odd jobs in order to take care of her young child. In these examples, it is difficult to separate the influence of gender and class, but clearly evident that both affect these women's lives in ways that are unrelated to their lesbianism.

Religion is another important axis of difference in identity that contributes to individuals' varied perceptions and experiences of different spaces and places. For instance, in describing differences between Minneapolis and St. Paul, one of the women was influenced by her identity as a Jew:

> I've generally found St. Paul the more liberal of the two cities. If you look back, there was a lot of anti-Semitism in Minneapolis, but St. Paul has a lot of diverse communities in it. I've always found St. Paul much more attractive primarily for that reason.

Another woman perceived the two cities differently, deciding that Minneapolis was the more "open-minded" community. Her religious identity and experiences were a large part of this decision. She had renounced her Catholic upbringing after losing a teaching post in a Catholic school because she was a lesbian, and she chose to live in Minneapolis because:

> . . . in St. Paul [all the lesbians] were in the closet because the Catholic church had a real big influence there.

These two women experienced the two cities quite differently, largely because they evaluated them not just as lesbians but also through their identification as members of other social groups.

Perceptions and experiences of living spaces are also shaped by race. One woman explained a housing decision that hinged on her race. She was renting an apartment in an area with a large African American population. The area was the site of a great deal of political activity and was being defined and celebrated as St. Paul's most visible and vital African American neighborhood. She decided that as a white person she was intruding on that emerging community, so she eventually moved out of the neighborhood.[2]

Identity is not singular, but rather, is contingent on many axes of difference, including race, class, gender, age, religion, and ethnicity. All these play a role in shaping one's life experiences and opportunities, as well as the meaning one attaches to these. So, while I focus primarily on the role of sexual identity in shaping living spaces, it is important to recognize that much of the heterogeneity in the meanings and constructions of these spaces emerges from each individual's unique identifications.

Just as lesbian identities are heterogeneous, so are lesbian communities. Within the scope of this project I have identified several different lesbian communities: the larger groups of lesbians occupying the Twin Cities area and beyond, smaller groups with shared social networks or whose members may be connected to the same cultural institutions, and still smaller groups defined by daily interactions and perhaps by shared living spaces. One of the women I interviewed captured these different layers of lesbian community when she observed,

> . . . you see, I'd always had a sense I knew who the lesbian community was, but I had no idea. I went to this [political organizing] meeting and there were women I had never seen before . . . who had their own social connections. It was something else . . . the women I lived and went out to the bar with, what I knew as the community was just A community, it wasn't THE [only] community.

These communities exist at a number of different scales. Like Anderson's (1991) discussion of national identity, a sense of lesbian "community" extends to include individuals who do not know one another or share social networks, but have a sense of unity derived from a common identity. But like Rose's (1990) discussion of community in a London neighborhood, lesbian "community" also includes the shared imaginings of individuals who interact on a daily basis, sharing physical and social spaces. These diverse communities are constructed in place, places which have many layers of meanings for the individuals who create and inhabit them. The living spaces of the home and neighborhood are as multi-faceted in their meanings as the individuals and communities who construct them. Feminist geography contends that the meanings of places are constantly changing, being formed and reformed by a shifting matrix of social, political, and economic forces. Individuals are simultaneously embedded in several discourses that constitute their identities and experiences in these places. It is this multiplicity of influences, experiences, and identities that is at the heart of shaping highly politicized lesbian living spaces that have many meanings for the individuals who create and inhabit them.

THE LESBIAN HOME-A SPACE FOR CONTESTATION

In examining the role of the home in African American culture, bell hooks (1990) introduces the idea of "homeplace." She writes of the personal and political significance of homeplace in African American experience, describing it as a place in which black women have been empowered to create and control a space where they and their families could be free from the domination and oppression of a racist society. She argues that the construction of a homeplace is a radically political act, because in creating a place in which one is subject, one resists an oppressive culture's attempts at objectification. Although the specific oppressions of racism and homophobia manifest themselves differently, the home can occupy a similar position of radical political contestation in lesbian experience. For many lesbian communities, the act of creating a homeplace is a refusal to be silenced in the face of a rigidly heterosexual culture.

These contestations take a number of different forms in lesbian homeplaces. When a woman creates a homeplace in which she is visible as a lesbian, she combats the social pressures that would marginalize and hide lesbian existence. Creating diverse families and households in these homeplaces challenges traditional heterosexual definitions of families. Using these homeplaces as important sites of identity formation and mutual support among lesbians further encourages the growth of oppositional identities and cultures. These struggles over spaces, both their meanings and societal expectations of the people, relationships, and activities they will contain, are what politicize the lesbian homeplace.

Contestation of heterosexual culture takes place when lesbians choose their homes as sites at which to assert their sexual identity to outsiders, rather than using their homes for concealment. In a society that demands that expressions of homosexuality be concealed from public view, some lesbians challenge this expectation. One lesbian household incorporated symbols of their lesbianism in their home. They flew a rainbow flag in their front yard and put up lesbian-related posters in their windows. Another participant used her home in the suburbs as a means to assert her lesbian identity publicly, refuse to be invisible, and bring diversity to her neighborhood. She said:

> So there I am for everybody to see, a dyke in the suburbs. I think it's good for the neighbors to see me–their world shouldn't be so straight. Every time a house goes up for sale, I try to get [lesbian] friends to move out here.

This woman battles lesbian invisibility in two ways, by refusing to "pass" as straight and also by striving to build a larger lesbian presence in her neighborhood.

Another woman told of a situation in which she used her home and objects in it to communicate her sexual identity to co-workers. When she held office gatherings in her home, she refused to remove artifacts that would clearly indicate to her co-workers that she was a lesbian. Visitors could see lesbian books and posters, a rainbow flag, and the absence of a second bedroom for the woman her co-workers had previously understood to be her "roommate." While she did not feel comfortable discussing her sexual identity at work, she had no objections to asserting her lesbianism in her home. This example supports hooks' (1990) argument that the home is a place where members of a minority group become subject rather than object. In her home, the woman described above takes the power of self-definition and assumes the right to be entirely open about her identity.

The previous examples, in which the home space is used to communicate one's sexual identity to others, do more than simply flout social pressures to keep lesbianism out of sight. When a lesbian uses her homeplace as a means to make her sexual identity visible, she blurs the boundary between public space and private space. Dominant discourse holds that sexuality, especially homosexuality, is to be hidden from public view and confined to private spaces.[3] Societal practice enforces this expectation, making performance of a lesbian identity outside the home difficult and dangerous. Lesbian constructions of the supposedly private space of the home highlight the difficulty of making clear and absolute distinctions between public and private spaces. In many of the living situations described above, the private space of the home is involved in articulation of lesbian identity in a way that is clearly and intentionally visible to outsiders. A sexuality that is supposed to be hidden inside the home instead is made apparent through that space in the symbols or objects displayed and through the relationships or activities that take place there. In these cases, the private becomes public.

While such open assertions of lesbian identity challenge societal demands for public invisibility of oppositional sexualities, any performance of lesbian identity, open or otherwise, is subject to close surveillance and sanction by a heterosexualizing culture. For instance, lesbians might face hostility from family or friends who visit their homes, or harassment from neighbors. Valentine (1993b) has documented how such surveillance can cause lesbians to change their behavior or remove symbols of their lesbianism from the home to avoid potential conflicts. Societal surveillance and the way it can limit expressions of lesbian identity also problematizes any fixed boundary between public and private space. The home is supposedly "private" space, a place of refuge from the prying eyes of "the public." But when social pressures of harassment or discrimination make the homeplace a barrier beyond which open expressions of lesbianism ought not venture, this assumption does not hold. Forces outside the home, embodied in societal disapproval or homophobic neighbors, are regulating the supposedly "private" space. The home space, ostensibly coded as private in modern capitalist society, becomes public in the sense that it is controlled in certain ways by external actors.

Lesbian homeplaces also challenge heterosexual culture by being sites for forming households that contradict more traditional expectations for the people or relationships which constitute "families." As Johnston and Valentine (1995) have argued, I also found that a wide and changing variety of situations are recognized as "families" or "households" within lesbian communities. These descriptions were offered by the women I interviewed:

> Myself and my partner Grace, another woman and her male partner, we lived in a two-bedroom apartment in town . . . the heterosexual couple broke up so he moved out and then it was Grace and I and Sharon. And Sharon moved out somewhere during that year and we ended up with an evolving succession of lesbian roommates . . .

> A bunch of us formed a cooperative household. We'd have gatherings for women looking for lesbian community. We'd invite women who lived alone to be sort of satellites to our family, so

> they could still live alone, but share a sense of community . . . then
> we started experimenting with income sharing and stuff like that.

> The woman upstairs was a lesbian and we formed like an extended
> family. We did things like take care of each other's kids. The doors
> to both houses were open and the kids went back and forth.

These families created within lesbian living space did not have a fixed
nor traditional form. "Family" did not necessarily imply a nuclear
family with children, one adult working outside the home, and one
adult maintaining the household.[4] Nor were these families always
established based on marriage ties or biological relationship. The co-
operative household even included individuals who did not live in the
same house. Some of these lesbian families and households formed on
the basis of intimate relationships. Others coalesced around friendships, shared political or social values, or mutual needs. These
women's homes were places where they created households that di-
verged from the traditional heterosexual expectations of family forms
and envisioned new ideas for the kinds of relationships upon which
family and community are based.

The lesbian homeplace is also a site of identity formation. In times
and places where lesbian bars and other public establishments have
been non-existent or unsafe, homes have provided an essential place
for nurturing lesbian identity. Kennedy and Davis (1993) and Johnston
and Valentine (1995), for instance, have described the importance of
gatherings in homes as an opportunity for lesbians to socialize together or make connections to a larger lesbian community. In these cases,
the lesbian homeplace is engaged in challenging dominant culture
because it is a place where oppositional sexual identities are built. The
women participating in this project talked about their homes in similar
terms. For many of them, living in households made up of other
lesbians was extremely important in shaping their identities. They
described how their house mates introduced them to other lesbians for
the first time when they were coming out. Those who already had
connections in the lesbian community expanded their circles of acquaintances through house mates. For some, their house mates held
social or political gatherings in their home and in this way they contacted other lesbians. One woman described how she and a house mate
began to explore lesbian culture together:

[My house mate] and I were both coming out during that time. So part of being in that house was that we were always talking about it and finding lesbian books to read and going to hear lesbian singers.

One of the older women explained that her home had re-emerged as her primary place for socializing. She no longer played sports with a lesbian team and she felt that the local lesbian bars catered to younger women. So she and her partner chose having gatherings in their home or going to the homes of others as their main social activity with other lesbians. In all of these instances, the home provides a place for building connections between lesbians, fostering a community of women who share a common sexual identity.

Not only is the home important as a place to nurture lesbian identities, for many of the women it is also a place to provide tangible material support to other lesbians. Establishing a home was a way for them to support other members of the lesbian community. Most rented from lesbians whenever possible. When purchasing homes, they tended to seek lesbian realtors to assist them. Although they also gave other reasons for these choices (like feeling "safer" or "more comfortable"), several explained that they wanted their rent or payments to a realtor to help financially support another lesbian. In a different example of this kind of support, one woman and her partner shared their house with a series of lesbians who were temporarily without places to live. She explained that this was their way of "helping the community." For many women in lesbian communities, the home is not a place where families are isolated from one another. Through the homeplace, the lesbian community is linked together both by formation of a shared oppositional identity and by mutual material support.

To this point, I have discussed lesbian homeplace in relatively liberating terms–as a place where many lesbians find community and affirmation, and as a place where they have the opportunity to confront, challenge, and redefine expectations of the dominant culture. This contrasts much of what has been written about lesbian experiences of home. Previous research has described the difficulties lesbians face in finding safe, affordable housing where they will not be harassed, and the tremendous efforts made by some lesbians to conceal their sexual identities from neighbors, families, and friends (Egerton, 1990; Valentine, 1993b). Johnston and Valentine's (1995) research describes how some lesbians living in heterosexual family homes challenge these pressures to hide their sexual identity by subtly inserting symbols of their identity into the home space. The women who participated in my project tended neither to actively hide their lesbian identity, nor to rely on subtle symbols in asserting their identity. Instead, through the symbols they choose and the homes they create, they tend to more openly defy assumptions of heterosexuality.

In spite of the openness these women displayed about their sexuality and the freedom many of them felt to challenge heterosexual expectations, in no way do I dispute previous work illustrating lesbians' oppressive experiences of home. The women I worked with still confronted many of the difficulties home space presents to lesbians, in spite of the opportunities they found for contestation. For instance, one of the participants was unemployed for a period of time and moved in with her parents when she could no longer afford her own home. Due to her parents' homophobia she could not be open about her lesbianism. Another participant described how she hid her sexuality when she rented apartments in St. Paul during a time when gays and lesbians had no legal protection from housing discrimination. In these situations, the women had limited power to create an affirming, liberating homeplace, or to use that space for contestation of heterosexual norms. An individual's experience of homeplace and control over that space in part depends on her having a certain degree of economic, social, or political power. Without such power, the home space can often limit a woman's expression of lesbian identity or her ability to connect with or create lesbian community. As women, sexual minorities, and possibly as members of other minority groups, lesbians are marginalized in ways that can make their homes constraining and oppressive.

A major factor in determining lesbian experiences of home is the social climate in the surrounding neighborhood. A lesbian home in an aggressively homophobic neighborhood is likely to feel more confining to its inhabitants than liberating. Not all lesbian homes exist in such a hostile environment, though. Many of the women who participated in this project lived in areas with relatively high concentrations of lesbians. Some had been moving among these areas for over twenty years, living in many different residences, but always living in a lesbian neighborhood. Like the lesbian homeplaces that are a part of them, these neighborhoods can contain a similar set of multiple and conflicted meanings. While the lesbian neighborhood is a powerful expression of lesbian self-definition and liberation, it can also be a place where lesbians are oppressed through harassment and discrimination.

Like the homeplace, lesbian neighborhoods can be places of affirmation, identity formation, and contestation of dominant culture. Some of the women I interviewed wanted to form visible lesbian communities to fight societal assumptions of universal heterosexuality. Others explained that their neighborhoods were important sites of lesbian political organizing and socializing. Another explained that living in a lesbian neighborhood was important because it was the only place she felt secure in being open about her sexuality.

These positive elements of the lesbian neighborhood exist alongside oppressive elements. A neighborhood that is generally recognized as having a large lesbian population might be a place in which lesbians are targeted for harassment. Even if most of the non-lesbian residents of such a neighborhood might be tolerant and accepting, lesbians still might encounter hostile neighbors or landlords. Many of the participants in this project were reluctant to talk about these more oppressive aspects of their homes or neighborhoods. Still, some of the choices they made about their homes indicated that they were responding to these potential difficulties. Most of the women, prior to renting or buying a home, made efforts to ascertain the potential reaction of landlords or neighbors. As other studies examining lesbian housing strategies have found, these women sought the advice of other lesbians, relied on for-rent notices in local gay and lesbian newspapers, or relied on the guidance of gay or lesbian realtors (Ettorre, 1978; Rothenberg, 1995). They avoided places where they perceived overt hostility and sought assurances that they would feel comfortable and secure in certain areas. As much as the lesbian neighborhood is a place of autonomy and a place where lesbians argue that they feel comfortable and secure, it is also a place in which they still go to great efforts to ascertain potential objections to their sexual identity. In spite of the fact that they can and do create a "safe" space in the lesbian neighborhood, this security is not total–they are still cautious of harassment and discrimination. The lesbians that live in these neighborhoods are simultaneously empowered by their own actions to create an affirming environment and constrained by real or perceived hostility from non-lesbian residents.

Another dual meaning of the lesbian neighborhood exists in the women's perception of the safety of their homes and neighborhoods. The most common explanation participants gave for wanting to have a home in a lesbian neighborhood was that these areas are "safer." This perception persisted in spite of actual incidents of harassment that occurred in the neighborhood. One woman was shouted at by a group of young men in a neighborhood park. Another had lesbian-related stickers on her car defaced outside her home. Another was evicted by a landlord who discovered her sexual identity.[5] Myslik (1994) found a similar situation among gay men. In his research in a prominent gay neighborhood of Washington D.C., gay men identified the neighborhood as a "safe" area but crime statistics showed a greater incidence of anti-gay crimes. Many equated feeling "safe" with being able to express their sexuality openly in a public place or with an area where they could be with other gay people. Thus, he argues that safety has a different meaning in homosexual experience. My own work supports this argument, but illustrates that safety has not just one, but several different meanings for lesbians.

The women who participated in this project defined a safe place as one in which they could be open about their sexual identity, whether this openness meant holding hands with a lover while walking in the neighborhood, or flying a rainbow flag on the side of the house, or organizing a lesbian picnic in the local park. If they felt comfortable doing these things, then they identified the place as safe, even if they were bothered by homophobic individuals in the neighborhood. At the same time, some also used "safe" in reference to places where they were confident of not being harassed. Another woman used safety in yet another sense when she said,

> . . . the neighborhood started getting kind of bad and we didn't feel safe. Not because we were gay, just because of crime. So I moved to a [different] house.

The connotation of the word "safe" and the meaning it takes on for lesbians changes when it is used in different contexts with respect to different social groups or various aspects of identity. At one point, the women were evaluating the safety of their neighborhoods with respect to themselves as lesbians. Their key concern in this situation was that other lesbians be present and that they feel comfortable being open about their sexuality. At the same time, like the woman quoted above, they might evaluate the "safety" of a neighborhood relative to all residents, not just lesbians. In the example given, safety took on a very tangible meaning and was defined by lack of threat from crime. The multiple meanings of the safety of a place seem to vary with the identity through which an individual is experiencing or analyzing that place.

If lesbians feel comfortable being open about their sexual identity within their neighborhood, then the neighborhood is an affirming "safe" place within which they might live freely without actively concealing their sexual identities. But if these lesbian neighborhoods and their residents are targeted for harassment or discrimination, the neighborhood is an unsafe and oppressing place. Thus, just as the lesbian homeplace can be a place of liberation and confinement, the lesbian neighborhood that surrounds it may also be simultaneously safe and unsafe.

CONCLUSIONS

Throughout, I have argued that lesbian living space is imbued with multiple meanings and realities. Spaces that are culturally coded as private in actuality are tightly controlled by dominant culture. Homeplace is both a place of liberation where lesbian identity and community are fostered and a site of oppression within which lesbian identity is frequently confined. The lesbian neighborhood is simultaneously perceived to be "safe" but is not actually free from actual or threatened discrimination. Lesbian living spaces are simultaneously situated at the center and the margin of social discourse. These spaces are the center for the lesbians who live and seek to form community there. This centeredness is both metaphorical and material. Lesbian living spaces represent symbolic places of safety, security, and community. But these spaces are also very tangible centers of many of the women's lives, the places they have lived, sought entertainment, and formed social networks and relationships of mutual support. From the perspective of dominant discourse, though, these spaces exist on the margin. So long as dominant discourse privileges heterosexuality, lesbian living spaces will remain socially marginalized.

This tension between the center and margin, between the home as a place of liberation and subjugation is the essential ingredient that makes the homeplace a space for lesbians to contest a culture that would make them heterosexual or invisible. For some lesbians, the home provides a certain base of security that is necessary for engaging in the challenge. The lesbian neighborhood and lesbian establishments can offer much the same thing–a sometimes-safe space to feel secure, to build community, and to temporarily avoid some of the battles members of a minority culture must face. But these spaces can also be part of a radical challenge of dominant culture. Whichever is the case (and this will vary in different times and places), these spaces are part of a highly politicized lesbian living space, a space through which lesbians influence and respond to the multi-layered power relations of our society.

NOTES

1. Exceptions include Peake (1993), Valentine (1993a), and Johnston and Valentine (1995).
2. All of the women in the group I interviewed were white. This is not reflective of the racial diversity of the Twin Cities' lesbian communities. I had great difficulty locating lesbians of color who had lived in the area for longer than four or five years. I am currently exploring other ways of locating a wider spectrum of the community, but at the time of writing I have not conducted any more interviews.
3. Scholars examining sexuality and space have argued that divisions between private and public are untenable. Valentine (1993a) shows that even though sexuality is supposedly limited to private spaces, heterosexuality is actively asserted in many public spaces. Peake (1993) shows that in lesbian experience, public spaces such as bars and bookstores are places where supposedly 'private' sexual identities are nurtured.
4. Indeed, some would say this formation is nearly extinct among heterosexual families in the U.S.
5. This incident occurred in the mid-1980s. Although attempts at repeal are ongoing, gays, lesbians, and bisexuals in Minnesota are now protected under a 1993 bill that included sexual identity in the state's equal protection laws.

REFERENCES

Sy Adler and Johanna Brenner (1992) 'Gender and space: lesbians and gay men in the city', *International Journal of Urban and Regional Research* 16, 1 pp. 24-34.
Benedict Anderson (1991) *Imagined communities: reflections on the origins and spread of nationalism* (Verso, London).
Jane Egerton (1990) 'Out but not down: lesbians' experience of housing', *Feminist Review* 36, pp. 75-88.
E. M. Ettorre (1978) 'Women, urban social movements and the lesbian ghetto', *International Journal of Urban and Regional Research* 2, 3 pp. 499-519.

bell hooks (1990) *Yearning: race, gender, and cultural politics* (South End Press, Boston).

Lynda Johnston and Gill Valentine (1995) 'Wherever I lay my girlfriend, that's my home: the performance and surveillance of lesbian identities in domestic environments', in Bell, David and Valentine, Gill (eds.) *Mapping desire–geographies of sexualities* (Routledge, London) pp. 99-113.

Elizabeth L. Kennedy and Madeline Davis (1993) *Boots of leather, slippers of gold: the history of a lesbian community.* (Penguin Books, New York).

Loyd, Bonnie (1982) 'Women, home and status' in Duncan, James (ed.) *Housing and identity: cross-cultural perspectives* (Holmes and Meier, New York) pp. 181-197.

Ruth Madigan, Moira Munro, and Susan Smith (1990) 'Gender and the meaning of the home', *International Journal of Urban and Regional Research* 14, 4 pp. 625-647.

Linda McDowell (1983) 'City and home: urban housing and the sexual division of space', in Evans, Mary and Ungerson, Clare (eds.) *Sexual divisions: patterns and processes* (Tavistock, New York) pp. 164-173.

Wayne Myslik (1994) 'Perceptions of safety: gay and lesbian communities of Washington, D.C.' Presented at the Annual Meeting of the Association of American Geographers, San Francisco.

Linda Peake (1993) ' 'Race' and sexuality: challenging the patriarchal structuring of urban social space', *Environment and Planning D: Society and Space* 11, 4 pp. 415-432.

Adrienne Rich (1989) 'Compulsory heterosexuality and lesbian existence', *Signs: Journal of Women in Culture and Society* 5, 4 pp. 631-659.

Gillian Rose (1990) 'Imagining Poplar in the 1920s: contested concepts of community', *Journal of Historical Geography* 16, 4 pp. 425-437.

Tamar Rothenberg (1995) ' 'And she told two friends': lesbians creating urban social space', in Bell, David and Valentine, Gill (eds.) *Mapping desire–geographies of sexualities* (Routledge, London) pp. 165-181.

Alan Ryan (1983) 'Public and private property', in Stanley Benn and Gerald Gaus (eds.) Public and private in social life (St. Martin's, New York) pp. 223-245.

Peter Somerville (1992) 'Homelessness and the meaning of home: rooflessness or rootlessness?', *International Journal of Urban and Regional Research* 16, 4 pp. 527-539.

Gill Valentine (1993a) '(Hetero)sexing space: lesbian perceptions and experiences of everyday space', *Environment and Planning D: Society and Space* 11, 4 pp. 395-413.

Gill Valentine (1993b) 'Negotiating and managing multiple sexual identities: lesbian time-space strategies', *Transactions of the Institute of British Geographers* 18, 2 pp. 237-248.

Flagrantly Flaunting It?: Contesting Perceptions of Locational Identity Among Urban Vancouver Lesbians

Jenny Lo
Theresa Healy

SUMMARY. The city of Vancouver has two overtly identified gay and lesbian areas: West-end, primarily perceived to be associated with men,

Jenny Lo is currently completing her Master's of Science at the University of Northern British Columbia in the Faculty of Natural Resources and Environmental Studies, Geography Programme. Her thesis research focuses on the service needs of women in resource-based communities in Northern British Columbia. She is also conducting research on economic restructuring and its impact on forest dependent communities.

Theresa Healy is currently completing her PhD in history at Simon Fraser University. Her dissertation focuses on the realities of women and families on relief in the 1930s. She is also currently employed as a sessional instructor in both the History and Women's Studies Programmes at the University of Northern British Columbia. She also works as the Executive Director of the Community Planning Council in Prince George and is involved with research on the quality of life in Prince George, which has included a survey on this issue for lesbians, gays and bisexuals.

Address correspondence to: Jenny Lo, Faculty of Natural Resources and Environmental Studies, Geography Programme, University of Northern British Columbia, 3333 University Way, Prince George, BC, Canada, V2N 4Z9.

Author note: We would like to thank everyone who contributed to this study. A special thank you to the people who helped get the word out and circulated information about this research. We are grateful to Anne-Marie Bouthillette for her generous assistance with some of the research material. A final thank you to the anonymous reviewers for their insightful comments on the earlier draft of this article.

[Haworth co-indexing entry note]: "Flagrantly Flaunting It?: Contesting Perceptions of Locational Identity Among Urban Vancouver Lesbians." Lo, Jenny, and Theresa Healy. Co-published simultaneously in *Journal of Lesbian Studies* (Harrington Park Press, an imprint of The Haworth Press, Inc.) Vol. 4, No. 1, 2000, pp. 29-44; and: *From Nowhere to Everywhere: Lesbian Geographies* (ed: Gill Valentine) Harrington Park Press, an imprint of The Haworth Press, Inc., 2000, pp. 29-44. Single or multiple copies of this article are available for a fee from The Haworth Document Delivery Service [1-800-342-9678, 9:00 a.m. - 5:00 p.m. (EST). E-mail address: getinfo@haworthpressinc.com].

and East-end, mostly identified with lesbians; thus, where the gender-ization of space and the sexualization of space converge, the urban lesbian and gay landscape is often gendered by spatial association. In reality, however, lesbian and gay enclaves exist outside these more popular locations and beyond the city peripheries and these two specific locations are not as neatly ordered as their mythical simplicity might suggest. This research explores the construction of lesbian spaces in metro Vancouver through extensive research which began during summer 1996, and the perceptions and expectations of lesbians living in both the East-end and the West-end of Vancouver will be examined. This introductory paper provides a discussion on the opposing views of lesbians in Vancouver expressed in the survey which explode commonly held myths and stereotypes of lesbians in the East-end and the West-end. In essence, lesbian residents hold opinions of the lesbians residing in the "other" community which have political and ideological implications. *[Article copies available for a fee from The Haworth Document Delivery Service: 1-800-342-9678. E-mail address: getinfo@haworthpressinc.com <Website: http:// www.haworthpressinc.com>]*

KEYWORDS. Lesbian, community, space, Vancouver

PREFACE: UNIFYING DIFFERENCES

If we were to amuse ourselves with stereotypical dichotomies, then these are more than met by the characteristics of the two researchers engaged in this study. Locational identity was only one of the differences marking the researchers. From young to old, Asian to Celt, androgynous to high femme, and more particularly, organized to chaotic, we can easily be identified as polaric clones; however, our commitment to forging greater academic depth in current research on lesbian geographies has translated differences into strengths. We are motivated by our shared perspectives on the lack of depth in writings on how lesbians construct their realities through space, as well as a desire to sustain our sanity in an often harsh and unwelcoming university environment.

As part of our attempt to redress this imbalance, our primary goal is a return to process, how research speaks with, to, and of lesbian lives. We are fortunate that, as we embark on this research with mixed feelings of passion and discontent at the lack of critical inquiry into lesbians' hetero-spatial identity, we have been met by insights, meanings and challenges provided by the participants in this research. As a result our research process is expanding to include triangulation and interactions with the participants throughout the research process: a process that marries both qualitative and quantitative principles.

CONTEXTUALIZING THE URBAN GAY LANDSCAPE

There is a growing collection of research on the comparative geographies of gay men and lesbians in urban areas. On a general scale, geographers have been preoccupied with studies that explore the overt gender differences between gay men and gay women in the city, in terms of how each adapts, adjusts and negotiates their daily experiences within dominant heterosexual urban space. In the past, geographers have identified a retreat into shared space or "buffer zones of sameness" (Levine, 1979). Since then, a lot of studies have critiqued Castells' (1983) premise of an exclusively gay male constructed urban space. Castells argued that lesbians have not constructed lesbian "ghettos" to the same extents as gay men because they do not, as women, have the same attachments to space as men (Lauria and Knopp, 1985; Alder and Brenner, 1992).[1] This assumption of an inherent gender difference between how gay men and women utilize and interpret space has been critiqued in recent work on lesbian landscapes by Valentine (1995) and Rothenburg (in Bell and Valentine, 1995). In particular, by revealing how Castells' discussion of the gay and lesbian population has perpetuated socially constructed gendered norms, many of the current studies provide an opposing argument on how lesbians occupy space in different cities. These lesbians' spaces have been described as taking many forms depending on the researchers' perspectives, such as 'placeless' (Castells, 1983), 'ghetto' (Ettorre, 1978; Valentine, 1995), 'quasi-underground' (Adler and Brenner, 1992) and 'counter-culture.' All these terms suggest that lesbians' spaces are not only different from gay men's territories, but that they are also more hidden and significantly less privileged. The space, described as invisible in Castells' work, is revealed by more recent work as subterranean and disguised.

Accessing this interstice of territory requires the advantages of a broad comparative research methodology between gay men and women. Specifically, this macro analysis can highlight the gender gaps and point to other social inequalities experienced by the gay population. A drawback of this gender comparison, however, is that it does not reveal significant insights that differentiate concerns for both men and women, regardless of sexual orientation. In fact, the conclusions from many of the studies only re-emphasize the urban issues faced by men, and women in particular, regardless of their sexual orientation. For example, regarding the issue of lesbians' lack of distinct territorial space, Adler and Brenner (1992) argued that several factors impinged, not only upon lesbians' ability to create lesbian-identified space, but also their abilities to make it as obvious and clearly defined as gay male space. Access to resources, providing for dependent children and fear of generalized violence against women restricted lesbians' choices and resources to create highly visible lesbian communities; however, the fact that women did create such communities, albeit of a lower profile than gay men, has been adequately detailed (Adler and Brenner, 1992; Lockard, 1985). As a result, then, comparative studies on gay men and lesbians often accentuate existing forms of gender discrimination by paying little attention to the heterogeneity within each group. It is apparent that what is lacking in 'queer geography' is an in-depth interrogation of lesbian-specific interactions within and across urban boundaries. For some urban lesbians who live in the midst of a predominantly gay male area, comparing the differences between gay men and women serves to sanction, silence and mask lesbian realities. The connectivity, tension and relationship experienced by lesbians living in different parts of the city may be overshadowed by a research process which focuses only on the obvious and overt gay male 'scene.'

One of the most perplexing aspects of the discussions on gay men and lesbians is the ambiguity of the term 'community.' This concept is defined and debated by different authors, each of whom emphasizes various aspects of the term. Although the gay population is often referred to as a 'community' within a larger heterosexual community, this concept becomes extremely complicated when references are also made to different aspects of 'sub-communities.' In her investigation of the production of lesbian spaces, Valentine (1995) applies Rose's (1990) concept of 'imagined communities' to refer to people's preconceived ideas of a named community. Rothenberg (1995), in her study on the gentrification of Park Slope in New York City, reviews various definitions of community used by scholars in different studies. Again, the concept of an 'imagined community' appeared to be a common reference for the gay and lesbian population.

Despite such ambiguities, a common aspect to the definitions of 'community' is the sense of a shared interest. It is common knowledge now that this sense of shared interest can be real or perceived. Our goal is to explore how lesbians identify their own lesbian communities by discursively situating themselves with other lesbians from different areas in the same city. This specific locational 'inter-identity' across space and place is rarely included in current studies.

It is still true, as Susan Krieger argues, that "basically we do not know very much, in the social sciences, about lesbian communities or about their interconnectedness with lesbian identity" (Krieger, 1982:10). As Sandoval (1984) goes on to point out, the social sciences have not developed the ability to map a broader lesbian experience other than that of a white, middle-class, urban feminist lesbian. The myths and meanings lesbians ascribe to their territory are explored here in a descriptive manner, focusing on the interventions of class and income on those ascriptions and the conflicting views of community that may develop within and across lesbian communities.

In Vancouver, there are at least two commonly recognized lesbian communities which hold opposing views from each other. These opposing views are rooted in perceptions of community and visibility. While West-end lesbians have tended to blend into the landscape of the West-end neighbourhood, East-end lesbians have, for the most part, publicly declared their sexual preferences on the landscape of the East-end. Ironically, while many West-end respondents mourned the absence of visible and out lesbians on the streets of their communities, the survey showed an inclination to look down on East-end lesbians for "flagrantly flaunting their sexuality."[2] In return, many East-end respondents viewed the West-end community as uninformed about the class and political issues of sexual identity politics.

POLITICIZING THE LANDSCAPE

A lesbian feminist perspective is useful in understanding how the heterosexually gendered, raced, sexed, aged, and the abled landscape (Chouinard and Grant, 1995) has impacted upon the lesbian's construction of space in metro Vancouver. Much research on where and why lesbians live where they do in urban areas has described lesbians as living in neighbourhoods similar to Vancouver's East-end (Valentine, 1995). In terms of understanding lesbian communities in

Vancouver, we argue that the prevalent stereotype of West-end is often understood as the 'male' landscape, and the East-end as the female landscape, and these are perceived to be two distinctly identified gay spaces. The West-end location is centred around Davie Street and the East-end around Commercial Drive (see Figure 1).[3] These two areas are the focus of this paper, though we must stress that such dichotomy does not include the reality of other lesbians living throughout Vancouver.

Although there are a mix of gay men and lesbians living in both neighbourhoods, these areas can be said to be gendered. The West-end is often associated with an image of 'boys' (gay men), 'yuppies,' wealth, clubs, materialism, trendy 'gay' fashion, singleness, carefree attitudes and a lack of 'family/household' responsibilities. On the contrary, the East-end, especially around the Commercial Drive 'lesbian ghetto' area, is perceived as a neighbourhood with lower economic status, co-operative housing, 'family'-oriented space, cultural

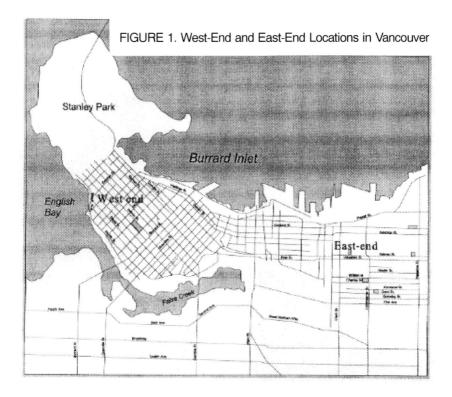

FIGURE 1. West-End and East-End Locations in Vancouver

diversity, less materialistic and greater socio-political awareness and activism, and a subaltern population. While there are indeed lesbians living in both the East-end and the West-end of Vancouver, the perception of a genderized queer space has glossed over the realities of lesbians who live and work in the West-end. This distorted illusion of a sexed and gendered space has great implications in terms of sustaining heterosexual hegemony (Valentine, 1993). There is an apparent ideological divide, and even tension, within the lesbian communities of the West-end and the East-end. As well, the prevalent view of the West-end, as a male-defined space, has significantly overshadowed and made invisible the realities of lesbians who call this area their home. This also trivializes the complexities of how lesbians view each other across the boundaries of these two locations.

LANDSCAPING THE RESEARCH PROCESS

The sample surveyed for this research describes the intricacies of lesbian-identified space. The West-end is primarily identified with gay men, but it also provides a sense of gay identity for a significant number of lesbians. This area is seen as materially advantaged, a seat of culture and art, and a place of action and activities in Vancouver as a whole. As one East-end respondent said of the West-end: "I perceive the west side as people who are more privileged–more white people– richer–more educated, More $ to do activities other than work and school."[4]

The East-end is said to be a poorer, working class, ethnically mixed neighbourhood, and is more readily identified as a lesbian "ghetto." It is perceived to be a politically radical neighbourhood, eclectic and diverse. As a West-end resident respondent reported her perception of the East side: "East Van is more interesting, has a more culturally diverse population, is less boringly trendy, has more community events that suit us, has nice older houses, is cheaper–BUT feels less safe for women who travel by bus." The Commercial Drive area may fit with what Adler and Brenner describe as 'quasi-underground.'

Research on this traditionally sensitive and ostracized community with conventional research methods does not allow us to interrogate issues in ways that are cognizant of and respectful towards contentious and critical areas. Moreover, these traditional methods reveal little about how lesbians 'create' space because our understanding of 'space' has been disabled by our censored perception of this 'non-conforming' and 'deviant' population. When we 'name' and associate particular 'spaces' within a city, the way we have defined marginal from acceptable and privileged space influences our research discussion. It is not enough, then, to simply apply traditional research instruments and practices in order to understand a once 'outcast' and 'suspect' population. What must be executed is a triangulation of traditional techniques with innovative and creative research methodology–a major goal of this project was to develop this combination.

Over the summer of 1996, advertisements were printed in community newspapers[5] and flyers were posted around Commercial Drive and Davie Street calling for volunteers to participate in an East-West survey. Other outreach methods included informational hand-outs at dances and Internet postings on lesbian discussion groups. In general, the response to the research was extremely encouraging. In fact, a consistent comment was to the effect that it was about time something was done. What emerged from our initial anecdotal experiences was a sense of division and alienation within the East-end and the West-end lesbian communities. There is a spatial tension reinforcing common perceptions of each area and intricately interwoven by the complexity of personal identity and community politics.

The information we have received has encouraged us to revise the time-line for this project. Not only are surveys still trickling in, but people who have only recently heard of the research are requesting surveys for themselves and friends. We are extending the process of seeking respondents, recognizing that the lower-income, ethnically diverse sector of the lesbian population is a difficult one to access by traditional research means. At present, we are in the process of reshaping and expanding the methods for outreach and recruitment; thus, the research is still in progress. We have found that a substantial collaborative effort is required in undertaking research among lesbians. Our experience with this project has taught us to rely on other lesbians almost as co-researchers rather than simply as respondents. Their connections to, and insights upon, their communities developed this work in ways we had not anticipated. As a result, we have an increased sense of accountability.

Comparing the number of surveys mailed out with numbers received, it is apparent that the respondents took it upon themselves to assist in this research by circulating photocopies of questionnaires to other lesbians.[6] This snowball method, although effective in increasing the number of responses, may have also skewed the sample to over-represent highly motivated people who are interested in the topic (Feitelson, 1991) or who understand the purpose and importance of surveys.

This commitment is apparent in the quantity and quality of responses in the surveys received. Respondents appear to have taken great time and care in answering, explaining, expanding and clarifying their responses. The concluding question of the survey, inviting respondents to expand on areas they thought we overlooked, became a source of information on the definition of community and issues of importance that we had not considered.

What we present here is an initial foray into the wealth of information created by this survey. We first outline the quantitative results for three of the issues related to perception of locational identity. We follow this with an analysis of these issues generated by the qualitative material.

SAMPLE PROFILE: DESCRIBING THE DESCRIBED

The sample of 35 respondents (we distributed a total of 60 surveys) presents a 40/60 divide between the East-end and the West-end lesbian communities in Vancouver. The predominant features of all the women responding to this survey are that the majority come from Anglo-Saxon backgrounds (85%), are in their early to middle ages (74% are between 25 to 45 years), have post-secondary education (97%), are involved in a long-term relationship (71%), and none have children living at home. In general, the women were "out" about their sexual orientation to most of their informal networks (see Table 1).

Based on the current sample size, there is only a small hint of a socio-economic divide between lesbians living in the East-end and the West-end. In looking at individual annual income, 37% of the sample population earn over $40,000 per year while 43% earn less than $20,000 per year. Among the higher-income earners, 77% live in the West-end; however within the lower-income group, there is less variation between women living in the East-end and the West-end (54% to 36%). Although access to economic resources has often been assumed as the sole determinate factor of residence (West-end for wealthier people, East-end for the economically disadvantaged), there are other

TABLE 1. Respondents "Out" to Formal and Informal Sector

Sector of community	% of sample out to sector
Close friends	100%
Immediate family	88%
Co-workers	80%
Extended family	65.7%
Neighbours	60%
School/University	25%
Others	22%

underlying locational perceptions which contribute to and influence lesbians' decisions to live either in the East-end or the West-end.

PERCEPTIONS OF EAST-END AND WEST-END

The Commercial Drive on the East-end of Vancouver is known, among the locals, not only as a place for cultural diversity, but also as a place that is 'non-mainstream' or an 'alternative' community. The resonance of 'The Drive' is that of a space which is accepting of those who do not conform but also thrives as a result of these same people.[7] That is, 'The Drive' is not simply a repository for marginalized peoples but a vibrant and empowered community. 'The Drive' has been described as 'funky' and interesting, and is also constructed as a place of resistance to dominant cultural norms (Bouthillette, 1995). This predominant image, however, glosses over the other realities that infringe upon individual choices. In our survey, we asked respondents to give their top three reasons for moving into the West-end or East-end (see Table 2). There was a clear difference in the top preference expressed by East-end and West-end residents. This clear demarcation between East-end and West-end residents as reasons for choosing their residential location may speak to the tyranny of economic realities for some lesbians in selecting residence, but may not be a primary factor for West-end lesbians.[8] For some lesbians other factors overrode economic reasons. Living with aging parents or living in close proximity to family members also determined residential location for some lesbians.

TABLE 2. Ranking of Top Three Reasons for Choice of Location

Ranking	Reason for Choice/East-End Respondents	Reason for Choice/West-End Respondents
First choice	Affordable housing (62%)	Relative location (41%)
Second choice	Affordable housing (38%)	Relative location (41%)
Third choice	Community and lifestyle (60%)	Community location (47%)

Some respondents, in spite of the appeal of lower rents in the East-end, choose to live in the West-end because of their perception of the East-end as "dirty," "crime ridden" and a generally unsavoury atmosphere. For these lesbians, the presence of 'flagrantly obvious' lesbians was a further disincentive: As one West-ender put it: "Many lesbians resent the male attitudes that relationships/love have to be sexually based, also most of my friends don't flagrantly flaunt their preferred sexuality . . . visibility does not represent my type of associates." Even for women who might find the East-end attractive, fear prevented them from locating there: "I love the Lez culture in the East-end and also the multicultural mix, shopping restaurants–way more affordable. I feel anxious there with the increasing violence/ threat."

The common theme for choosing the West-end, however, was "location, location, location." This neighbourhood was seen as central to everything desirable: night life, beaches, galleries, theatres and attractive businesses. Nevertheless, the primary focus of many businesses and services in the West-end is the gay male and the upper-class wealthy and hip heterosexual. One East-ender summarized the West-end as "[t]oo pretentious, too 'showy,' too many boys, too costly to live there. Although it's nice to be by the beaches and other conveniences like shopping." The overall West-end atmosphere is perceived to be culturally and materially rich. Within this flamboyant materialism, the West-end lesbian is much less successful at proclaiming visibility to herself and other lesbians.

For some East-end lesbians, in spite of incomes that could comfortably accommodate the higher rents of the West-end, the attractions of 'The Drive' were stronger. Some critical components for lesbians choosing to live in the East-end included the sense of neighbourhood, the visible lesbian community and the alternative lifestyles that seem welcomed and vital to the neighbourhood.

While an individual may have expectations that are met, perceptions may well change. We asked respondents to assess whether their perceptions of their community changed since they started living there. In the East-end few (2 of 13) believed their perceptions had changed since they moved into the neighbourhood. Among West-end respondents there was a greater shift. Seven of the 22 respondents believed their perceptions had changed, while the rest did not think their perceptions had changed. Our analysis is that the West-end community is far more ephemeral and amorphous for lesbians, thus distorting perceptions of potential residents as to its nature. Due to the more flagrant nature of the East-end, potential residents' initial perceptions are far more concrete and explicit and more likely to be reinforced rather than challenged by experience. Overall, this experience with initial perceptions may reinforce general stereotypes the two communities hold of each other.

Of those respondents who believed their perceptions had changed, we explored how, and in what ways. There was a clear contrast around two issues in this regard. Respondents from both the East-end and the West-end of the city identified issues such as diversity, increasing conservatism or evidence of injustice with no real discernible differences between the two communities. The sense of community and lesbian visibility proved a stark difference (see Table 3).

The sense of community identified by East-end lesbians is rooted in several factors. First, the East-end community covers a smaller area and is consequently more dense in population. The neighbourhood as represented by local businesses is, on the whole, welcoming to the lesbian population. From vegetable markets to Italian coffee shops, from commercial establishments to economic alternatives such as co-ops, the visible lesbian appears as an equal and valued citizen in the community. Further, the lesbian is perceived as a dynamic presence that adds an attraction and vitality to the urban street scape.

The West-end experience, on the other hand, is mediated by other

TABLE 3. Perception of Community and Lesbian Visibility: By Location and Number

Location of Respondent	Sense of Community	Lesbian Visibility
East	6	0
West	0	3

factors. Covering a larger territory, scattered and divided by an up-wardly mobile lifestyle. The occupation of urban space by a clearly identifiable body read as 'lesbian' is obliterated in the 'hip' image that marks the West-end. Respondents in the East-end felt their community was more friendly and had a greater community spirit than had been expected. West-end respondents expected greater lesbian viability in the neighbourhood than they found and consequently desired the pres-ence of the missing lesbian bodies on their streets even though they decried the presence in the East-end.

CONCLUSION

This paper is not about making any specific claims for the Vancouv-er lesbian community at large because of some very real limitations to the study. For example, although small, the sample is representative across a broad range of areas, such as age and income, but the sample is limited in some important respects. No respondent in our sample has children, the sample is predominantly Anglo-Saxon and the total num-ber of respondents is small. These drawbacks suggest necessary changes to our work. For example, the sample frame and identification were focused on the lesbian population of neighbourhood and as-sumed accessibility for all lesbians. Assumptions do not assure acces-sibility. It is clear that future survey distribution will have to be further refined to focus on ways to enter the various sub-communities within the lesbian community at large. That is, in spite of desires to the contrary, our survey proved exclusionary rather than inclusive. The information by respondents to date, however, does suggest some fruit-ful lines of enquiry on notions of locational identity.

This paper explores the perceptions among lesbians in two distinct urban gay areas in the city of Vancouver. Combining the concept of a visible presence decoded as lesbian with perceptions and expectations reveals some important understandings of a locational identity framed by oppositional and contradictory ideas. The community spirit gener-ated in the respective communities was rooted in the notion of visible presence, the markings of a lesbian body on the neighbourhood.

There is a political dimension to this discussion. In the East-end, lesbians have used their bodies to write and mark their presence on the landscape, to identify and claim territory. They have reinforced a particular visual identity that communicates a sense of difference from the broader community. West-end lesbians do not occupy urban space with the same spirit. In this predominant gay male space, lesbians are less apparent to each other and to other lesbians living outside the West-end as only one facet of their identity and, for some of these, not the primary element. These lesbians appear to be critical of the East-end lesbians who live there because of their perception that East-end lesbians are "flagrantly flaunting" their sexual orientation. At the very same time, they mourn the absence of the visible lesbian on their own streets. East-end lesbians, on the other hand, embrace this identity, calling themselves on occasion: 'East-end Bad Girls.' When East-end lesbians critique those living in the West-end, they tend to focus their criticisms on the general ambience of the West-end, ascribing those characteristics to the lesbians living there.

Still, among these two polaric opposites are lesbians who resist the locational impositions and negotiate a shared space that is both and never East or West. This initial research, like many other studies, dispels Castells' notions of lesbians' disassociation with space and territory.

While this study is still evolving, the wealth of detail generated by this survey opens up several other avenues requiring investigation. In particular, the different household structure and the extended, informal support of non-heterosexual people should be studied in relation to the geography of non-traditional families. As well, in exploring the construction and the constructs of lesbian communities, it is important to explore the creation of communities and the interplay between lesbians actively seeking out a place of belonging and a space of identity. There is a minefield of work waiting on how lesbians use symbolic markings on their own bodies–their own territory–and in turn use the body to mark the urban landscape. Furthermore, there may be a correlation between where lesbians choose to live and the life-stage at which they are 'out.' Finally, it would be worthwhile to examine the linkages between lesbian, women and citizen issues in the community, as each are not contingent upon the other, and they do not necessarily intersect. While this study began by outlining the two demarcated lesbian landscapes in the city of Vancouver, we have learned that beneath this surface facade there are conflicts within the minds, bodies and spaces of communities that are multiple, complex and contested beyond the simple dichotomy that lesbians themselves may perceive.

NOTES

1. We use the term 'gay' to refer to both homosexual men and women when referring to general lifestyle issues, but we use 'lesbian' in the more specific context.

2. All quotations are drawn from the qualitative sections of the surveys.

3. These areas are identified and mapped in the *Gay and Lesbian Business Directory*, an annual publication produced by Chaorus Publications and the Gay and Lesbian Business Association. For the purposes of this paper, the common definition of the West-end, that area bounded generally by Davie, Denman, Robson and Granville Streets, also includes some responses from the West Side, i.e., Kitislano and Point Grey. The map in Figure 1 is provided courtesy of Anne-Marie Bouthillette.

4. The quotations used here reproduce the language and symbols exactly as presented in the surveys.

5. Advertisements calling for participants were printed in two well-circulated gay and lesbian newspapers, *Angles* and *Xtra-West!* The survey incorporated both quantitative and qualitative questions and included a space at the end for an open-ended comment. Each survey also included a separate, unattached sheet asking for volunteers for follow-up, in-depth interviews.

6. While the research population undertaking to distribute the survey themselves is a sign of involved and empowered respondents, the researchers have to ensure that the survey tool is designed for subjects who take the research into their own hands. That is, the survey must be designed to include all information necessary to inform each individual receiving it as to the nature and terms of the research.

7. An example of the nomenclature can be seen in Cindy Filipenko, "To thrive on the Drive," *The Buzz*, Oct. 1996, pp. 16-17.

8. Locational refers to proximity to amenities. Affordable housing refers to affordable rents, real estate and access to co-op housing. Community and lifestyle, the third choice for both residents in the East-end and the West-end, refers to elements such as proximity to friends, people of similar sexual orientation and entertainment choices.

REFERENCES

Sy Adler and Johanna Brenner (1992) Gender and space: lesbians and gay men in the city, *International Journal of Urban and Regional Research*, 16, pp. 24-34.

David Bell and Gill Valentine, (eds.) (1995) *Mapping desire* (Routledge, London).

Anne-Marie Bouthillette (1995) Queer scapes: patterns and processes of gay male and lesbian spatialization in Vancouver, B. C. MA thesis, Department of Geography, University of British Columbia.

Craig Calhoun (1994) Separating lesbian theory from feminist theory, *Ethics*, 104, pp. 558-81.

Manuel Castells (1983) *The City and the Grassroots* (Edward Arnold, London).

Vera Chouinard and Ali Grant (1995) On being not even anywhere near 'the project': ways of putting ourselves in the picture. *Antipode*, 27, 2 pp. 137-166.

Tim Davis (1995) The diversity of queer politics and the redefinition of sexual identity and spaces, in Bell, David and Valentine, Gill (eds.) *Mapping Desire* (Routledge, London) pp. 284-303.

E.M. Ettorre (1978) Women, urban social movements and the lesbian ghetto. *International Journal of Urban and Regional Research*, 2, pp. 499-520.

Eran Feitelson (1991) The potential of mail surveys in geography: some empirical evidence. *Professional Geographer*, 43, 2, pp. 190-204.

Cindy Filipenko (1996) "To Thrive on the Drive" *The Buzz*, 1, 1, pp. 16-17.

Susan Krieger (1982) Lesbian identity and community: recent social science literature. *Signs*, 8, 1 pp. 91-108.

Laura, M. And Lawrence Knopp (1985) Toward an analysis of the role of gay communities in the urban renaissance. *Urban Geography*, 6, pp. 152-69.

Martin Levine (1979) Gay ghetto. *Journal of Homosexuality*, 4, pp. 363-77.

D. Lockard (1985) The lesbian community: an anthropological approach. *Journal of Homosexuality*, 11, pp. 83-95.

Tamar Rothenberg (1995) 'And she told two friends . . . ': lesbians creating urban social space, in Bell, David and Valentine, Gill (eds.), *Mapping desire* (Routledge, London) pp. 165-181.

Chela Sandoval (1984) Comment on Krieger's 'lesbian identity and community: recent social science literature,' *Signs* 9, 4 pp. 725-729.

Gill Valentine (1995) Out and about: geographies of lesbian landscapes, *Journal of Urban and Regional Research*, 19, 1 pp. 96-111.

_____ . (1994) Toward a geography of the lesbian community. *Women and Environments*, 14, 1, pp. 8-10.

_____ . (1993) (Hetero)sexing space: lesbian perceptions and experiences of everyday spaces, *Environment and Planning D: Society and Planning*, 11, pp. 395-413.

The Virtual Spaces
of Lesbian and Bisexual Women's
Electronic Mailing Lists

Celeste Wincapaw

SUMMARY. The lesbian and bisexual women's electronic mailing lists of the Internet have created electronic lesbian and bisexual spaces which simultaneously reflect and yet differ from real-time lesbian spaces. This paper summarizes data collected in a 1995-96 survey in which over 100 subscribers of the lesbian and bisexual women's mailing lists answered both qualitative and quantitative questions about the interface between their on-line and real-time lives. As is reported in this paper, many of the survey respondents sought lesbian and bisexual on-line spaces where they could avoid men and heterosexuals but, in order to do so, had to negotiate the sometimes-difficult terrain of electronic co-existence with a diverse group of lesbians and/or bisexuals. This diversity caused difficulties for some survey respondents which mirrored many of the difficulties of their real-time lives. Yet, the impetus was also planted for the development of identity-specific electronic mailing lists where like-minded lesbians and/or bisexuals could enjoy affirming

---

Celeste Wincapaw completed the research for this article as part of her Master's thesis for the ever-patient and queer-friendly Department of Geography, Carleton University, Ottawa, Canada. Celeste is currently employed by a Vancouver-based feminist organization. Her passionate debates include comic book heroes, IRC (Internet Relay Chat) addictions, garbage-picking, and on-line flirts with her real-time partner, Mary Henderson.

Address correspondence to: Celeste Wincapaw, BC Centre of Excellence for Women's Health, E-311 4500 Oak St., Vancouver, BC V6H 3N1, Canada (e-mail: celeste.wincapaw@bccewh.bc.ca).

[Haworth co-indexing entry note]: "The Virtual Spaces of Lesbian and Bisexual Women's Electronic Mailing Lists." Wincapaw, Celeste. Co-published simultaneously in *Journal of Lesbian Studies* (Harrington Park Press, an imprint of The Haworth Press, Inc.) Vol. 4, No. 1, 2000, pp. 45-59; and: *From Nowhere to Everywhere: Lesbian Geographies* (ed: Gill Valentine) Harrington Park Press, an imprint of The Haworth Press, Inc., 2000, pp. 45-59. Single or multiple copies of this article are available for a fee from The Haworth Document Delivery Service [1-800-342-9678, 9:00 a.m. - 5:00 p.m. (EST). E-mail address: getinfo@haworthpressinc.com].

communication and interaction. *[Article copies available for a fee from The Haworth Document Delivery Service: 1-800-342-9678. E-mail address: getinfo@ haworthpressinc.com <Website: http://www.haworthpressinc.com>]*

KEYWORDS. Lesbian, mailing list, bisexual, on-line space

There are "real time" lesbian spaces of the bar, the k.d. lang concert, or the North American softball field; spaces inhabited by real, smelling, living, breathing, desire-ing lesbian bodies. These are spaces where women often get information about other women based on the outward appearances of their bodies, clothing, and personal mannerisms. Many lesbians try to "fit" in these real-time spaces by adopting or *performing* their lesbian identities. This *performance* can be thought of as doing, dressing, living, fucking, or generally being whatever one thinks of as "lesbian." For some women this might mean wearing a particular t-shirt. For others it might mean frequenting certain "lesbian" locales such as the local women's pub. For others, it could simply (or not so simply) mean affinity or identification with a historically-contingent and contextually-specific word such as *lesbian*.

For many of the women interviewed for this article, words such as *lesbian* and *bisexual* were used to electronically search for ways to meet other lesbians and bisexuals. These words were used as direction signs to particular types of Internet space, virtual lesbian spaces.

VIRTUAL LESBIAN SPACES

Virtual spaces are not readily visible features of the cultural landscape; they do not have street addresses and cannot be found on standard maps. Instead, they are created by an electronic intellectual or emotional connection via the written word and an electronic medium. They are the spaces created by, amongst other means, certain application of the Internet such as electronic mailing lists. An electronic mailing list, sometimes called a listserv, allows subscribers (and, if it is an open list, non-subscribers) to broadcast messages to everyone on the mailing lists.[1] On some mailing lists, these broadcasts are used as a sort of one-way communication. For example, an employer might use a mailing list to communicate directives to employees, especially those in various locations. Yet, on other lists, namely on many of the lists for lesbian and/or bisexual women, the mailing list becomes a place where many people send out broadcasts to the entire list and create a *space* of sorts for lesbian and or bisexual conversation. They are electronic meeting places, or *virtual space,* where people who may or may not identify as either lesbian and/or bisexual have the opportunity to discuss or listen to discussions about lesbian and bisexual lives.

Internet scholar Steven Jones says that the concept of a *virtual* reality is something which people *seem to need* but it is *"hardly less 'bewildering' than non-virtual reality"* (Jones, 15). Jones writes that sometimes virtual spaces are similar to and sometimes they differ from real time spaces. Yet, he says, referring to virtual communities, *"They form a new matrix of social relations"* (Jones, 15).

Jones also writes that the socially produced space of computer mediated communication gives people mobility. They can "visit" places without ever traveling. They can also *"have mobility of status, class, social role, and character"* (Jones, 17).

The former, the mobility of virtual traveling, is important in the on-line lesbian and bisexual communities, particularly for those persons who live in places where they don't have the real-time support and companionship of lesbian and bisexual women. The second type of mobility, as described by Jones, can also be experienced by participants in lesbian and bisexual women's virtual spaces. For example, some participants might not identify as "lesbian" or "bisexual" in their real-time lives but might choose to "try on" those identities in virtual, on-line spaces.

DATA COLLECTED VIA E-MAIL

The information contained in this article was gathered as part of a survey of lesbian and bisexual mailing list participants. In the fall of 1995, advertisements were circulated via electronic mail to mailing lists which the author identified as being primarily for lesbians and/or bisexual women. The advertisements were mailed to the list owner who then decided whether or not the advertisement should be posted on her list(s). The vast majority of the list owners contacted were very willing to post the advertisement to their lists.

The advertisement asked that list subscribers circulate it amongst other lesbian and bisexual mailing lists. The reason for this was that the author wanted to include those mailing lists which were very private, invitation-only lists for which no list owner/moderator could be readily contacted. Approximately 200 people responded to the advertisement. Of the responses, only one was disqualified from participating because she didn't meet the criteria of the survey. Of the remainder, approximately 100 people returned completed questionnaires and "signed" letters of consent.[2]

The questions asked of the participants ranged from basic demographic questions to qualitative questions which asked respondents to define terms in their own words or to explain how they felt about a particular topic such as electronic co-existence of lesbians and bisexuals on the LISTS. The responses to the approximately 38 qualitative and quantitative questions were coded and then entered into a database which allowed the author to calculate quantitative data and at the same time allowed the author to search the large volume of qualitative data with coded keyword searches. Some of the survey respondents replied with pages of text, others with one-word answers. Approximately 15 people initiated follow-up correspondence about the project. This correspondence consisted of 1-5 e-mail messages between the author and the respondent. The content of those messages was directed by the respondent and usually focused on whatever areas of concern the respondent had about the survey. These follow-up conversations were organized by topic, coded and entered into the project database but were only reprinted with permission of the respondent.

The survey responses were then analyzed in order to study the interface between the real lives and actions of the survey respondents and their participation in the electronic spaces of the LISTS. Specifically, this project explored the differences and similarities between the survey respondents' on-line, electronic experiences and their real-time, everyday lives.

The particular type of virtual space considered for this article, the lesbian and bisexual women's electronic mailing lists (LISTS), are virtual spaces created by electronic social interactions. These interactions are based on a loose affiliation within and across lesbian (and bisexual) communities. There are also LISTS for black lesbians, Jewish lesbians, sober lesbians, fat lesbians, academic lesbians, and many others. For some women, the LISTS are important because they provide places to meet women with like identities. For others, the LISTS are important because they provide opportunities to explore and develop ideas about identity. Yet for others, namely bisexuals, the LISTS, or at least a specific LIST, can be an important space of refuge from a lesbian world which can sometimes be as hostile, and even more discriminatory, than the rest of the world.

Using the technology of the Internet, lesbian and bisexual women have created or co-opted over two dozen electronic mailing lists.[3] These mailing lists create forums, or *spaces* which are uniquely lesbian and/or bisexual women's spaces. There are an ever-changing number of electronic mailing lists, all of which specifically state that they are intended for, but not exclusively populated by, lesbian or bisexual women. In explaining why she wanted to be a part of the LISTS one lesbian wrote,

> *I really wanted to connect with other lesbians and to have something queer-related to read during the work day (. . . I worked in ultra straight environments).* (survey respondent)[4]

In the context of the LISTS, the words "lesbian," "bisexual women," and "woman" are often left open to individual interpretation, but "lesbian" usually refers to women who have an erotic attraction towards other women while the words "bisexual women" usually, but not exclusively, refer to women who might but do not always have the capacity for erotic attraction toward both women and men. The word "woman" sometimes refers only to persons who were born with female genitalia and other times includes transgendered persons.

A study of the lesbian-oriented electronic mailing lists of the Internet showed that very few LISTS limited subscription to lesbian women without somehow making a statement about the definition of the word "lesbian." Some lists were open to lesbians and to the "lesbian side" of bisexual women; that is, bisexual women were allowed to participate if they refrained from discussing their romantic relationships or sexual activities with men. Other lists were open to lesbians or bisexual women but did not welcome lesbian transsexuals. Other lists were open to lesbians, bisexual women, and post-operative transsexual lesbians. Yet another list was open to anyone who self-identified as either lesbian or bisexual but no definition of either of those two words would be provided so potential subscribers were free to define and interpret those words for themselves. This complete self-identification made a place for people who did not want a sexual label. It also made a place for persons with biologically male bodies or heterosexual identities to assume a lesbian or bisexual woman's identity.

AVOIDING MEN AND HETEROSEXUALS

There are an estimated 2,000-5,000 list subscribers, many of whom identify as either lesbian or bisexual women, who use the electronic mail forum of the LISTS to converse amongst themselves without interacting with either males or heterosexuals. Many of these LIST subscribers feel strongly about these places where they can openly talk about their lives as females and as sexual minorities in a world dominated by male heterosexuals. *"In a patriarchal and homophobic world,"* writes one lesbian LIST subscriber, *"women-only spaces feel safer and friendlier, and they allow me to connect with other women with whom I share what I perceive as a fundamental attribute: a love of women"* (survey respondent).

As distinctly *female* homo-sexualized spaces, the LISTS are also important, primarily because they are perceived as safe places for lesbians, and to some degree bisexual women, to talk about their lives without negative interference from males.[5] As one LIST subscriber explained it,

> *We don't have to listen to pig men try to dominate and harass us.*
> (survey response)

In addition to providing spaces where heterosexuals are in the minority, the LISTS create spaces where lesbian and bisexual women can talk amongst themselves without interacting with gay males. This makes the LISTS different from many other places on the Internet where due to economic power, level of comfort with technology, or perhaps lesser or differing risks associated with public visibility, gay males have created very visible and very male-oriented spaces. These spaces often take the form of personal advertisements or sexually explicit materials which did not interest many lesbian or bisexual women. *"I just get so sick of reading about one seven inch, cut throbbing hunk of meat seeking another,"* writes one lesbian LIST subscriber, *"where are all the burning clits seeking perky breasts? Or maybe lesbians just don't go about it like that"* (survey respondent).

Another woman also expressed frustration with the lack of knowledge most of the LIST participants seemed to display about Internet etiquette but is willing to overlook it in exchange for some personal attention from other women. She wrote,

> *(I'm) not interested in 100 messages a day of one-line flirts (not directed at me:-)*. (survey respondent)

The survey respondents were, generally speaking, women who knew a lot about computers and the Internet. Unlike the general female population, quite a few were students or were employed in the computing, scientific, and technological industries. Also, quite unlike the general female population, there were almost no manual, domestic, or unpaid household laborers and very few retail or service workers. While certainly not representative of women as a whole, these women were in unique positions; they were using technology as a way to communicate and thereby subvert the dominant forces of heterosexuality.[6]

While this one survey of only 100 LIST participants could in no way provide any indication of the ways in which the entire population of LIST subscribers are employed, it does demonstrate that those who participate in the LISTS were probably comfortable with computers before they joined the LISTS. It also clearly indicates that many of these women had the skills, resources, and confidence necessary to utilize other Internet technologies but they were choosing not to do so because they didn't want to interact with men or heterosexuals.

AVOIDING MEN, NOT MASCULINITY

In the context of a study on lesbian and bisexual women's experiences of the Internet, any concept of gender must go beyond subsuming lesbians and bisexuals under the categories of either "female" or "woman." One must theorize lesbian and bisexual as more than just another variation of "woman." Lesbians and bisexuals can be distinctly and simultaneously "woman" and "non-woman." That is, lesbians and bisexuals can interpret and define the concept of "gender" to fit their individual needs at a particular time and place. As Phelan writes of recent lesbian theories,

> *While retaining "lesbian" as a meaningful category they have worked against the reification of lesbians and toward views of lesbianism as a critical site of gender deconstruction rather than as a unitary experience with a singular political meaning.* (Phelan, xvi)

As there are no real-life characteristics which prove one's sexual preference, there are no foolproof methods of determining these via the Internet. The person they are speaking to might be a heterosexual woman "trying on" another sexual identity. The person might also be male. They might be transsexual. They might be a person who self-identifies as a lesbian but sleeps with men. Or they may be a sexually "vanilla" lesbian pretending to be an all-knowing, whip-flashing dominatrix. One never really knows.

On the LISTS, there are no visual cues as to the gender identification of its participants but by changing her name or assuming a pseudonym, a woman can "speak" in a masculine way and also assume a male identity on the Internet. Women can experience the positive aspects of being male, like being taken more seriously in conversation. Spender writes,

> *Gender-blindness at least holds the possibility of being able to leave behind the baggage that goes with being rated as a female speaker.* (Spender, 244)

Spender writes that women who are harassed or put down for speaking as women cannot take on a more masculine way of speaking without being subject to even more harassment. *"We are all aware,"* writes Spender, *"of the double standard that allows the same words to be masterful if coming from a man, but are domineering, bossy, aggressive–even castrating–if they come from a woman"* (Spender, 243).

What is missing from Spender's analysis in *Nattering on the Net: Women, Power and Cyberspace*, is the recognition that lesbian and bisexual women's spaces and in particular, the spaces of the LISTS, are markedly different from the Internet as a whole.

Lesbian and bisexual women embody a complex combination of both masculine and feminine characteristics. Many lesbians and bisexuals consider themselves to have masculine and feminine characteristics; these persons, sometimes called androgynes, make up the majority of lesbians and bisexual women on the LISTS. These modern androgynes tend to value both the masculine and the feminine aspects of another woman and are probably not going to harass a woman who speaks in a strong, straightforward, domineering, and what Spender calls a "masculine" manner. Some might comment on the word choice of the masculine female writer but some might even admire the writer as they admire someone who can fix a car, program a computer, or do any other traditionally masculine task.

Many lesbian and bisexual women joined lesbian and/or bisexual women's electronic mailing lists because they are seeking to interact with other females. They are not deciding that they do not want to interact with masculinity because, most likely, there will be some very masculine lesbians and bisexual women on the list.

Some lesbians and a few bisexual women describe themselves as "butch" and will acknowledge that they are, indeed female but might not think of themselves as a woman. The masculine woman (sometimes called a butch), has often risked harassment in heterosexual spaces for her daring ability to dress and act like the societally powerful heterosexual male. She opens herself to the risk of harassment usually only from other heterosexual males who feel threatened by her. Therefore, the situation of the proudly visible butch will be very different on the LISTS than it is amongst heterosexuals. On most of the LISTS, especially those designed for the butch and her admirer, the ultra-feminine femme, she will be accepted or possibly revered for her masculine ways.[7]

POLICING IDENTITY

There are no fool-proof procedures or a singular set of guidelines which allow only the lesbians and bisexual women to participate in the LISTS. Usually, in order to subscribe, one must first find the directions to do so. Some of those directions are well-advertised, usually by other lesbians or bisexual women, on the Internet and in print media. Other lists are relatively unadvertised. Once one finds and executes the commands for subscription, one must usually wait for the approval of the list administrator. The list administrator usually asks the potential subscriber to answer a few questions and, on the basis of the potential subscriber's response to those questions, decides if the potential subscriber can subscribe to a list. Some administrators use their technological skills to check at least the most basic aspects of the list subscriber's identity. *"I try to keep a sharp eye,"* writes one list administrator, *"and I use some list admin. tools to learn a lot more about people than they think I can discover"* (survey respondent).

Other list administrators do not want to check the identities of potential subscribers. *"If someone says they're a woman I have to believe them,"* writes one lesbian list moderator, *"I don't have the time to police people's gender identities. For that reason my list is open to all women, including transgendered women"* (survey respondent).

Differences amongst LISTS moderators make the boundaries of the lesbian and bisexual spaces of the electronic mailing lists highly permeable in some places and almost impossible to penetrate in others. The personal advertising strategies of the LIST moderator and the LIST participants control and direct the visibility of the LISTS. Some lists are not advertised at all but recruit members via word of mouth (or computer) only.

Most subscribers know that if anyone threatens or overtly harasses another LIST subscriber, they will usually be forcibly removed from the LIST. Yet, despite the possibility of harassment, most of the 100 list subscribers surveyed for this article said that they were never harassed by someone who knew them via the Internet but should they be harassed were prepared to fight back or retaliate. *"If someone harassed me,"* wrote one lesbian, *"I'd post the offending material to everyone on the LIST and then we'd all gang up on him"* (survey respondent).

SAME SHIT, DIFFERENT MEDIUM

The LISTS can be seen by some as a refuge from the male-dominated, heterosexual world but to others, notably for persons of color, fat women, older women, women with specific religious beliefs, or women who have controversial views on sexual practice, the LISTS re-inscribe the often discriminatory and usually intolerant practices of the rest of the world. *"Same shit, different medium!"* said one woman who self-identifies as a "fatdyke" (survey respondent).

The majority of the respondents to this survey were white, well-educated, and considered "race" to be a non-issue in their experiences on the LISTS. Many women of color had a different experience, one in which race was, indeed, important. *"I can see why,"* wrote a black lesbian, "*a group of mostly white, educated middle-class women wouldn't see racism. Race itself doesn't come up until one of 'us' walks in the room. I also believe, based on experience, that people–especially articulate folks–are presumed white until proven otherwise*" (survey respondent).

And yet, if a person of color does decide to identify themselves as such on the LISTS, they face the same kind of racism as in real life.

> *What I've experienced is a discounting of black womyns' experience within the community of womyn-loving womyn–both on-line and in the hardworld.* (survey respondent)

Therefore, faced with the racism prevalent on many of the LISTS, women of color choose to create their own separate lists as places where they could connect with women with similar experiences. Perhaps to create a space where, as bell hooks says, black women's rage against white women can be expressed

> *. . . for transforming internalized anger into constructive, self affirming energy.* (hooks, 109)

Electronic connections can also create a black community for those persons who live in white neighborhoods or cities. Said one black woman,

> *(I) needed to communicate with other African American L/B/T (Lesbian, Bisexual, Transsexual) women. Hey, I'm the only out black dyke in this white city of 44,000.* (survey respondent)

While certainly there is racism directed toward black lesbians and bisexuals, there are also positive aspects of multiple identities. As Houston writes,

> *Women of color view their ethnic cultures as sources of joy and pride, not simply as sites of sorrow and agony.* (Houston, 50)

THE GREAT BISEXUAL DEBATE

Persons who attempt to make a sharp division between the identities of lesbian and bisexual will soon recognize that people can call themselves both or neither, depending upon the context. Persons who choose to focus on either the words "lesbian" or "bisexual" as linguistic signifiers must recognize that the discursive power of these words is contingent on ever-changing, inconsistent, and socially constructed meanings.

The inclusion of both lesbians and bisexual women in this project reflects the reality of most lesbian and bisexual women's electronic lists; spaces where lesbians and bisexual women often co-exist. This co-existence is not without problems but it is happening and, unlike many lesbian-dominated spaces, bisexual women are not subsumed under the category "lesbian."

It is extremely problematic to define categories based on the differences between lesbians and bisexuals. It is not something which can be based on sexual activity because lesbians can have sex with men and still call themselves lesbians while bisexual women can have sex exclusively with women and still retain a bisexual identity. Second, the catch-all term "bisexual" somehow implies commonality amongst bisexuals which thereby privileges sexual identity over other aspects of identity. Certainly some bisexual women may have more in common with straight women or lesbians of a particular race or class than they do with bisexual women of differing race or class.

It could be asserted that reluctance to call one's self "bisexual" is particularly strong amongst lesbians in environments or organizations which are hostile to bisexuals. As an unidentified bisexual woman recorded by Armstrong says, *"No bi woman I know has escaped the pain of being ostracized by some elements of the lesbian community"* (Armstrong, 199).

The question of how lesbians and bisexual women can co-operate or co-exist is one which is important for society as a whole and certainly for this project. When asked what they thought about co-existence on the LISTS, there was a very mixed response amongst the survey respondents, of whom over half self-identified as "lesbian" and approximately twenty percent identified as "bisexual." Almost all of the bisexuals said that they could easily share the LISTS with lesbians but approximately 20% of the lesbians didn't want to share the LISTS with bisexual women. *"The lesbian-focused lists,"* writes one bisexual woman, *"do require some self-censorship for bisexual women, since we know that our romantic/other involvements with men are not discussions that are welcomed"* (survey respondent).

One lesbian said that she didn't think that lesbians and bisexuals should co-exist on the same list because

Lesbians and Bi's have different agendas and that *some* if not all lesbians are offended especially when the Bi's talk about their male partners. (survey respondent)

Although there is no singular bisexual identity, many bisexual women believe that love and sexual attraction are not contingent on the sex of a person. These bisexual women say that the traits they seek in a person are socially-constructed and can be found in men or women. Most of the bisexual women surveyed indicated that they had a distinct preference for women and quite a few stated that they were in committed relationships with women, yet by self-identifying as "bisexual" they are acknowledging that the have been or could possibly be attracted to persons of either sex.

CONCLUSION: LIST SPACES

Many of the LIST subscribers joined the LISTS in order to find a place where they could make a connection with other lesbians and/or bisexuals. Of the women who responded to this survey, the majority reported only very positive LIST experiences. They had found electronic friends with whom they could discuss politics, sports, sex, and a host of other subjects. A few had even found partners via the LISTS. Yet, there was also a substantial number of survey respondents who said that they experienced the same kind of discrimination and lack of consideration on lesbian and/or bisexual lists as they did in real-time lesbian spaces and in the heterosexual world at large. These persons noticed that due to systemic inequity based on, amongst other things, race, class, gender, and sexual practice, certain persons have more societal influence and power, both in the world as a whole, and in the cultures of the LISTS.

In this way, it is important to remember that while the LISTS allow subscribers to decide what they will and will not reveal about themselves, there are still racist, classist and sizist assumptions, amongst others, on the LISTS. Therefore, on most lists, when a list subscriber chooses to reveal certain aspects of their identity, they might be subject to the same lack of understanding on the LISTS as in real life.

Yet, specific LISTS can also be places of refuge, strengthening, and political organizing for those working against discrimination of all sorts, both in real time and on the LISTS. The LISTS provide a place where people can get the strength to cope with and to fight against specific oppressions. So, for example, a lesbian woman-of-size can join a LIST of fat lesbians and get some fat-positive support. She might also find information from other LIST subscribers about how to fight against fat oppression.

By articulating some of these ways in which "real time" identities affect the meaning of these virtual spaces (and vice versa), the dialectical nature between sexual identity and sexual space is enriched with the reminder that distinctly female homo-sexualized space is simultaneously a refuge from homophobic or misogynist intolerance and yet it can also be a vehicle for oppression against lesbians or bisexuals of certain races, sizes, or ethnicities. As a result of these societal oppressions, many lesbians and bisexual women, particularly those marginalized by racism, have fewer comfortable Internet spaces than heterosexuals. In this way, the new virtual spaces of the Internet are nothing new.

NOTES

1. The word *listserv* is defined by authors Gilbert and Kile as "a basic e-mail list." Yet, it is technically a type of e-mail list. The electronic mailing lists referred to in this article were created by Majordomo, listserv, and other types of mailing lists.

2. The letters of consent were "signed" electronically with either the person's real name or their e-mail address.

3. The names and contact information for the mailing lists are not provided in order to protect the locale of the research. This omission of locational information was done out of consideration for the persons and LISTS involved in this project.

4. McDowell writes about "straight" or heterosexual working environments.

5. Bisexual women cannot speak freely about all aspects of their lives on many LISTS. Due to the bi-phobia of some lesbians, bisexuals often only discuss their male partners (if they have one) on lists dedicated to bisexual women.

6. Light discusses her vision of women as proactive, empowered users and creators of Internet technologies.

7. While this survey did not focus specifically on butch/femme, many of the survey respondents spoke on the subject. Kennedy and Davis discuss butch and femme in their history of a lesbian bar community.

REFERENCES

Armstrong, Elizabeth. (1995) "Traitors to the Cause? Understanding the Lesbian/Gay 'Bisexuality' Debates" in *Bisexual Politics: Theories, Queries, and Visions*, Naomi Tucker (ed.) New York & London: Harrington Park Press, Inc. pp. 199-218.
Gilbert, Laurel and Crystal Kile. (1996) *Surfer Grrrls*, Seattle: Seal Press.

hooks, bell. (1994) *Teaching to Transgress*, New York & London: Routledge.

Houston, Marsha. (1992) "The Politics of Difference: Race, Class, and Women's Communication," in *Women Making Meaning, New Feminist Directions in Communication*, Lana F. Rankow (ed.) New York & London: Routledge. pp. 45-59.

Jones, Steven G. (1995) *Cybersociety, Computer-Mediated Communication and Community*, London: Sage Publications.

Kennedy, Elizabeth Lapovsky and Madeline D. Davis. (1993) *Boots of Leather, Slippers of Gold, The History of a Lesbian Community*, New York: Routledge.

Light, Jennifer S. (1995) "The Digital Landscape: A New Palce for Women." *Gender, Place and Culture*, V. 2, N. 2.

McDowell, Linda. (1995) "*Body Work, Heterosexual Gender Performances in City Workplaces*," in *Mapping Desire* David Bell and Gill Valentine (eds.) New York & London: Routledge. pp. 75-98.

Phelan, Shane. (1994) *Getting Specific, Postmodern Lesbian Politics*, Minneapolis & London: University of Minnesota Press.

Spender, Dale. (1996) *Nattering on the 'Net: Women, Power, and Cyberspace*, Toronto: Garamond Press.

And Still, the Lesbian Threat:
or, How to Keep a Good Woman a Woman

Ali Grant

SUMMARY. The regulatory fictions of sex and gender have been implicated in the maintenance of a compulsory heterosexual order and gender hierarchy. Through a consideration of particular geographies of oppression and resistance–local white feminist anti-violence activism–this paper illustrates some of the concrete manifestations of the deployment of these fictions in the regulation of gendered performances. By presenting certain aspects of political activism as 'UnWomanly Acts,' it is suggested that the frequent marginalization and displacement of politicized lesbians and other transgressive females in specific locations reduces the potential of these as sites of resistance, whilst simultaneously shoring up the regulatory power of the terms *lesbian* and *woman*. The paper hopes to add to projects of re-assessment and re-alignment current in anti-oppression struggles, by reaffirming the threat that multiple lesbian identities continue to pose to heterosexual hegemony across space. *[Article copies available for a fee from The Haworth Document Delivery Service: 1-800-342-9678. E-mail address: getinfo@haworthpressinc.com <Website: http:// www.haworthpressinc.com>]*

KEYWORDS. Lesbian, anti-violence, activism, transgression, regulation

---

Ali Grant has recently completed a PhD at McMaster University, Canada. Her thesis is entitled "Geographies of oppression and resistance: Contesting the reproduction of the Heterosexual Regime."

Address correspondence to the author via e-mail (ali@lightspeed.bc.ca).

[Haworth co-indexing entry note]: "And Still, the Lesbian Threat: or, How to Keep a Good Woman a Woman." Grant, Ali. Co-published simultaneously in *Journal of Lesbian Studies* (Harrington Park Press, an imprint of The Haworth Press, Inc.) Vol. 4, No. 1, 2000, pp. 61-80; and: *From Nowhere to Everywhere: Lesbian Geographies* (ed: Gill Valentine) Harrington Park Press, an imprint of The Haworth Press, Inc., 2000, pp. 61-80. Single or multiple copies of this article are available for a fee from The Haworth Document Delivery Service [1-800-342-9678, 9:00 a.m. - 5:00 p.m. (EST). E-mail address: getinfo@haworthpressinc. com].

What would lesbians know about sexual assault? Who would be assaulting them?

–John Prentice, Hamilton-Wentworth regional councillor
(Peters 1993b)

INTRODUCTION

In November 1992, a women's shelter in southern Ontario, Canada, ran an ad for a relief and child-care worker. The ad included the following commonly-used employment equity statement: "applications [are] particularly encouraged from lesbians, racial minorities, aboriginal and francophone women" (Tait 1992: B6). Members of local Rotary Clubs quickly threatened to withdraw a $500,000 pledge (for a new 20-bed shelter) and joined several regional councillors in demanding that the shelter explain what the category "lesbian" was doing in the ad. Halton Women's Place (the shelter) quickly apologised, stating a mistake had been made and that all future ads would simply indicate that they were "an equal opportunity employer." The shelter, and the pledge, survived the controversy (Longbottom 1992).

However, when an almost identical controversy erupted less than two months later, over nearby Hamilton Sexual Assault Centre's use of similar wording, the reaction of that women's organization was very different. Its executive director stated that there would be no apology for the inclusion of "lesbian" in the ad, arguing that "you don't back down from a position you feel is right because your funding is threatened" (Peters 1993a: B1). Local representatives from municipal government, social service, feminist, and lesbian and gay organizations, became involved in a protracted public debate over the validity and intention of the inclusion of "lesbian"; before too long, the first of several anonymous complaints arose (via the local media) about the Centre being "anti-men," "anti-police" and having a "lesbian bias." The Centre could only weather the storm so far before "asking" its three main funders for an organizational review.

These and several other events surrounding local feminist anti-violence activism in the early 1990s suggested that despite the popularity of lesbian chic, despite k.d., Melissa and the ubiquitous "gay" storyline in prime time, the lesbian threat was alive and well and living in southern Ontario. In this paper, I draw on doctoral research[1] conducted during 1991, 1992 and 1993, to briefly illustrate one of several interconnected processes which operated to regulate and contain organized anti-violence activism in and around the city of Hamilton,[2] Canada during that time. By suggesting that feminist anti-violence activism–as a set of counterhegemonic ideas and practices which challenge the current gender system–constitutes "UnWomanly Acts," I illustrate ways in which the process of "deradicalization" can be understood, in part, as a punitive consequence of feminist anti-violence activists and/or organisations not "doing gender right" (Butler 1990).

MAPPING THE HETEROSEXUAL REGIME

Radical lesbian Monique Wittig (1992: 27) argues that:

> although it has been accepted in recent years that there is no such thing as nature, that everything is culture, there remains within that culture a core of nature which resists examination, a relationship excluded from the social in the analysis–a relationship whose characteristic is ineluctability in culture, as well as in nature, and which is the heterosexual relationship.

This is undoubtedly true of the discipline of Geography which has been relatively slow in its uptake of questions of sexuality, especially heterosexuality. Its resistance to critical lesbian and feminist interventions reflects the persistence of a hegemonic masculinity in the discipline (Johnson 1994; Longhurst 1995; Pratt and Hanson 1994; and Rose 1993). Two decades or more of feminist geographies have gone a long way to challenging this state of affairs; still, it is only in the last few years that lesbians have begun to carve out some intellectual and political room in the discipline of the spatial (Bell and Valentine 1995a; Grant forthcoming; and Valentine 1993a, 1993b, 1993c). As stronger connections between lesbian and feminist geographies are slowly forged, there is hope for an end to the "ongoing non-examination of compulsory heterosexuality in geography" (Johnson 1994: 110).

Lesbian and gay geographies have emerged as a critical, exciting area of research. In their edited collection, *Mapping Desire*, David Bell and Gill Valentine (1995a) provide a comprehensive review of this literature; suffice here to note that by the mid-1990s there has been a relative explosion of work on heterosexuality as regulatory, on the body as a site of oppression and resistance, and on the performance and regulation of sexed and gendered identities (e.g., Bell and Valentine 1995a, 1995b; Chouinard and Grant 1995; Cream 1995; Duncan 1996; Keith and Pile 1995; McDowell and Court 1994; Peake 1993; Pile and Thrift, 1995). This work has, of course, been influenced by a wide range of post-colonial and post-modern writings as well as work in cultural studies and there has been fairly broad recognition in feminist, lesbian and gay geographies, and beyond, of the politically constructed nature of the category Woman (Gibson-Graham 1994; Nicholson 1990). This has involved a re-thinking of central analytical and political categories such as sex, gender, femininity and masculinity (Bell et al., 1994; Knopp 1995; Kobayashi and Peake 1994; Probyn 1995). Monique Wittig (1992) and Judith Butler (1990) in particular, have made influential and convincing cases for the consideration of the categories of sex (Woman/Man) as only making sense within a regulatory heterosexual system. That is, within white, Western society, the political regime of heterosexuality (Wittig 1992) is the system whereby humans are categorized as either female or male; these two categories, and bodies, must be sexually attracted to each other, clearly different from each other, and display certain behaviours and desires. That this system is in fact a *system,* or regime, is masked through its naturalization and through the characterization of transgressions, such as lesbian existence, as unnatural and abnormal. As lesbian theorist Marilyn Frye (1983: 34) has argued:

> For efficient subordination, what's wanted is that structure not appear to be a cultural artifact kept in place by human decision or custom, but that it appear *natural*–that it appear to be a quite direct consequence of the facts about the beast that are beyond the scope of human manipulation or revision.

What Women are *taught* to be, through repetitive, disciplinary and regulatory messages and processes, simply becomes what Women *are.* As Judith Butler has illustrated, gender is "a construction that regularly conceals its genesis" (1990: 140).

I want to suggest that one way to *map* the contours of the heterosexual regime, those ideological and material processes whereby it is produced, reproduced and contested, is through an investigation of spaces and struggles of resistance in and against it. For example, in sexual assault centres and shelters, feminist anti-violence activists often move beyond the limits of acceptable Womanly praxis by challenging the system of men's violence against females.[3] Like the more obvious and direct "subversive spatial acts" (Bell and Valentine 1995a) of groups such as the Lesbian Avengers and ACT UP, which expose the manufactured nature of (hetero)sexed space, feminist anti-violence activism exposes the limits of the heterosexual regime by directly contesting men's rights vis-à-vis women (in Canadian society) and by challenging the "proper doing of gender" (Butler 1990). By thinking of men's violence against females as one of the processes used in the manufacture and maintenance of an oppressive gender hierarchy, we can think of feminist anti-violence activism as a direct challenge to that process. In investigating various ways in which females contest the boundaries of acceptable Womanly behaviours, desires, attitudes, activities, and employment, the power relations, practices and ideas which work to order society as heterosexual (and therefore as a gender hierarchy) are uncovered. An obvious example is lesbians who come out; we risk various forms of material and ideological disciplining and punishment, including loss of friends, family, credibility, employment, and housing and/or threats, harassment, ridicule, and violence. Less obviously, feminists (lesbian or not) who challenge the "place(s)" of Women (for example, as appropriate targets of men's violence) are identified as *unfeminine, loud, brash, unwomanly, angry, unladylike, unsatisfied, frigid, manhaters* and *dykes*– all beyond what Women should be. In refusing to "do gender right," to be a Woman, to do the things Women should do, behave the ways Women should behave, feminist activists can constitute a cardinal transgression in the heterosexual regime. Females who transgress, materially and symbolically, become UnWomen.

If we think of traditional sites of feminist and/or lesbian activism as spaces of political resistance in and against the heterosexual regime, the struggles over both what types of activism will go on in these particular spaces and how these spaces are regulated (externally and internally) can be understood geographically. That is, the form and outcome of these struggles *matter* for identity formation in place, and for local capacities for political mobilization. Activists' individual and collective experiences of resistance and subjection to heterosexual rule, and their understandings of these experiences, affect the possibilities for different types of spaces to be ones of resistance or incorporation. It affects their capacities in place, for challenging the material and ideological processes of the political regime of heterosexuality, and an investigation of anti-violence activism on the ground, so to speak, can clearly illustrate ways in which the fiction of gender is effectively deployed to keep women being Women.

FEMINIST ANTI-VIOLENCE ACTIVISM: CONTESTING GENDER

That brand of feminist anti-violence activism which contends that men choose to use violence, that they use it because they can (culturally) and that for the most part they get away with it, exposes the reality that men can use violence against their own women (wives, daughters, nieces, lovers, domestic workers, prostitutes) with less risk of sanctions than when they use it against other men's women (mitigated, of course, by other systems of oppression) and/or other men.[4] This type of feminist activism attempts, to greater or lesser degrees, to contest Men's right to *be* and thus the reproduction of the heterosexual regime. The rules and regulations of the heterosexual regime operate, albeit in contradictory, complex and contestable ways, to punish and discipline certain types of practices and ideas that most clearly transgress the boundaries of what is intelligible in a society ordered on a woman/man dualism.

This different way of imagining can allow for a mapping of feminist activism as UnWomanly Acts; illustrated, for example, by the "lesbian question" and "man question." That is, activities that effectively challenge the naturalness of the heterosexual regime (whether real or imagined, for example, rape crisis centres "turning women into lesbians" or being "man-hating") are condemned by funding bodies and "the public." In order to maintain legitimacy, feminist organizations such as shelters and rape crisis centres must often illustrate what they are not: (a) they must not be lesbian; and (b) they must not be disloyal to men (e.g., "anti-men," "anti-police"). The lesbian threat is, of course, a classic way of controlling the limits of Women's capacities to contest the reproduction of gender hierarchy. As Marilyn Frye (1992: 124-125) writes, "the message . . . is clearly that a woman who is a feminist or does anything or betrays any attitude or desire which expresses her autonomy or deviance from conventional femininity is a lesbian." I want to suggest that many analyses of the "deradicaliza-tion" of organized anti-violence activism, in which rape crisis centres and shelters have often been transformed from their previous place as *the* sites of radical organized challenges to men's violence to state-controlled centres of service provision, have missed an important piece of the puzzle through their lack of attention to the role that the "lesbian threat" and normative gender scripts have played in the regulation of the more radical aspects of the movement.[5]

This deradicalization, locally and elsewhere, has to be viewed in the context of a conservative backlash in Canada against any progressive social movements. In the case of feminist anti-violence activism, there has been a contradictory situation in which violence against women has had a high public profile during the late 1980s and into the 1990s, but anti-feminist sentiments have become a common and acceptable component of contemporary public discourse and practices. December 6th, 1989 was a defining moment in this developing discourse, in that across Canada, most women will remember what they were doing and where they were when they heard that an armed man, shouting that he hated *feminists,* targeted and slaughtered fourteen women at L'école Polytechnique in Montreal. As one local activist noted, "Every woman I know remembers the minute they heard about Montreal and the reaction they had . . . It just serves to keep us in line" (activist 14[6]). Ruth Roach Pierson summed up what many feminists argued in the subsequent national debate over the meaning of the violence, when she argued that the gunman's

> . . . targeting of fourteen young women cannot be separated from widespread and socially validated hatred and fear of women in general, that his targeting of female engineering students cannot be separated from widespread and culturally validated resent-ment of "uppity," "pushy" women who enter fields once mo-nopolized by men, and . . . his anti-feminism cannot be separated from widespread media attacks on "strident," demanding femi-nists. (1990: 10)

Debra Black (1991) discussed several high-profile events on Cana-dian university campuses which illustrate this anti-feminist trend. For example: barely one month before the massacre in Montreal, the date-rape awareness program at Queen's University in Kingston, Ontario, was mocked by male students who placed signs in the windows of their dorm stating "No Means Dyke," "No Means Tie Her Up," and "No Means Kick Her In The Teeth"; in the fall of 1991, also at Queen's, the eight female editors of a newspaper received an anonymous death threat reading, "Here's your politically correct death notices. We're gonna rape u dykes . . . in fact, we will kill any and all feminists slowly"; and, the graffiti "Dyke Propaganda" defaced the 1991 date-rape awareness campaign posters at the University of Toronto, Ontario (Black 1991). The conflation of *dyke* and *feminist* is obvious in all incidents. By contesting the naturalness of the gender system, in which females are seen as appropriate targets of men's violence, feminist anti-violence activists, lesbian or not, disrupt the limits of the category Woman. As Debbie Wise Harris (1990: 40) argues, in an analysis of several of these acts, "in a dangerous twist, or inversion, the contemporary discourse is situated in a kind of 'post-feminism' where out-moded concerns of feminists rightly lead to hostility against them." This was certainly evidenced locally.

AND STILL THE LESBIAN THREAT . . .

Hamilton's Sexual Assault Centre, then, was only one of several local organizations mired in controversy in the early 1990s (see Grant 1996). After a period when both feminist activism (especially anti-violence activism) and men's violence against females were very high profile, the local community entered a particularly tumultuous period. Feminist anti-violence activists had been heavily, and very publicly, critical of various state institutions including the police and the legal system, especially through two high-profile cases. First, the case of Guy Ellul. On the first anniversary of the Montreal Massacre (December 6, 1990), a Hamilton jury acquitted Guy Ellul of a charge of first-degree murder in the death of his estranged wife Debra. The acquittal, based on self-defence, was handed down despite the fact that Ellul had stabbed Debra 21 times and left her to be found dead the following morning by her mother, Ruth Williams. Women's groups in the city were outraged and representatives formed a group to meet with the provincial Attorney General to demand an appeal of the decision. Out of that group the Justice For Women Coalition was born, a radical direct action and advocacy group with an individually-based membership of women's advocates and survivors. The Coalition organized to seek justice in the Ellul case; however, one year following the acquittal, the Ontario government announced that they would not, in fact, appeal as promised. Although government lawyers had filed their intention to appeal on the grounds that the jury was not properly instructed by the judge on the law of self-defence, they had done this within the first month of the decision (as required), and had since decided against the appeal on the grounds that they could find no errors in law (Brown 1992a; Tyler 1992). Justice For Women organized another protest and support rally outside the courthouse in which they believed justice had not been served, and in early January, 1992 they launched the Justice For Debra Campaign (Justice For Women 1992). Over the next year and a half, a red rose[7] was lain on the statue outside the courthouse every day by a member of Justice For Women. During the same period, Ruth Williams, Debra's mother, conducted a daily vigil outside the courthouse. Despite broad-based local, provincial and national support and publicity, which included numerous local and provincial rallies, letter-writing and petitions, Ruth Williams did not receive justice (Casella 1992; Davy 1992a; Deverell 1992; Prokaska 1993a and 1993b).

Second, the case of Larry Fodor. An investigative report by the city's newspaper, *The Spectator*, revealed the Hamilton-Wentworth Police Department's treatment of an officer who had broken his wife's nose in an assault (Holt 1991). Constable Larry Fodor had received a suspended sentence, probation and counselling for alcoholism and aggression, after pleading guilty to a charge of common assault against his second wife. The report outlined the policeman's checkered history and the ensuing controversy over his treatment was fuelled by the reported comments of his boss:

> Hamilton-Wentworth Regional Police Chief Robert Middaugh says he has no misgivings about Fodor handling domestic disputes. "I have no qualms about putting him back on the street," Middaugh said, noting that two officers are sent to every domestic call and that a supervisor monitors all such incidents. Using an analogy, the chief said "Who better to send to talk to an alcoholic than another alcoholic?" (Holt 1991: A1)

Justice For Women, with broad representation and support from local women's groups, organized a press conference where they called for a review of the Hamilton-Wentworth police department by the Ministry of the Solicitor General. They argued that the "police departments and the courts colluded to protect an officer from bearing the full penalty of his crime" (Marlin 1991: A1). The coverage of the press conference in *The Spectator* was accompanied by a photo of a workman removing spray-painted graffiti from the United Empire Loyalists statue in front of the county courthouse downtown. The slogans "Justice For Women Now!" and "Police Protect Their Own!" were being removed. The following day, the executive director of the Sexual Assault Centre was arrested, charged with public mischief under $1000, and released. The day after that, the police arrested, charged with public mischief under $1000, and released a counsellor in the Family Violence Program of Family Services of Hamilton-Wentworth. Both activists were members of Justice For Women. In the first of several support rallies organized by the group, they stated:

> Women of the Hamilton-Wentworth community are asking why police take such swift action to punish acts of resistance and protest by women while turning a blind eye to Officer Fodor's violation of his female partner's human rights to safety, security and justice.[8]

The alleged disparity between the police treatment of the women involved and of abusive men was evident when it came to the court proceedings. That is, despite paying for the cost of the clean-up, having no previous criminal conviction and over 20 years combined involvement in community struggles, the activists were found guilty as charged and ordered to spend 30 days in jail or each pay a fine of $500 (Lefaive 1992a). A member of Justice For Women noted that "the most common punishment for wife assault in this community is either a conditional discharge or a fine of $300," pointing out that the protesters had received harsher punishments than abusive men normally do (ibid. B1).

Nonetheless, Justice For Women continued to publicly criticize the police and legal systems. In August 1992, they called for assistant crown attorney Toni Skarica to be removed from domestic violence cases after it had been reported in *The Spectator* that he had decided to clear a court backlog of bail hearings (Brown 1992b; Davy 1992b). Skarica, who had failed to win a conviction in the Ellul case, was concerned that there was a backlog due to a blanket policy of "no release" for anyone involved in a domestic violence case. Skarica was temporarily removed from domestic violence cases but quickly reinstated after an internal review (Lefaive 1992b). Obviously, feminist anti-violence activism was playing a very visible and significant part in local urban politics. In September, however, *The Spectator* (1992) ran an editorial critical of the Justice For Women Coalition. Entitled "A wider vision," the editorial took aim at "special interest groups" with an "axe to grind":[9]

> In Hamilton, recently, the Justice for Women Coalition complained bitterly about statements made by assistant Crown Attorney Toni Skarica about bail hearings. As a result, Mr. Skarica was temporarily removed from prosecuting domestic assault cases, pending an investigation which cleared him of the outrageous suggestion that he was somehow anti-woman. The fact that a lobby group was able to cause such hardship to Mr. Skarica shows an undue influence. The fact that his superiors bowed to this is equally worrisome. (ibid. A8)

By November, the first lesbian ad controversy surfaced, followed quickly by the one involving the Sexual Assault Centre. Obviously there were a range of factors involved in shaping these particular struggles and reactions to them (see Grant 1996); however, one of these was undoubtedly the deployment of the regulatory fiction of gender through the "lesbian threat." As this activist pointed out:

> In many people's eyes, I am a lesbian, or any feminist is a lesbian and as far as the media are concerned they can assassinate a whole bunch of women, lesbian or not, by just calling them that and I think that's what the media are into right now in a big way . . . you are a threat to the patriarchy, off with your head sort of thing. (activist 15)

This comment points to the fact that "lesbian" as a regulatory term, signifies much more than a sexual identity. "Lesbian" is often used as a code word for a host of other terms which operate to reduce the legitimacy of the person at whom they are directed; the most common of which are "anti-male," or "manhating." That is, it is not women having sex with other women in and of itself that is regarded as a threat to the heterosexual regime, but the independence of females from men; this independence illustrates materially that the organization of society into Women and Men is neither "natural" nor "immutable." As Constance Durocher (1990: 16) explains:

> By refusing to have sexual relationships with men, lesbians es-
> cape from an important aspect of appropriation in the private
> sphere: they avoid the physical and mental control that men exert
> on women in their private lives. If lesbians, who are part of the
> class women, escape from certain major forms of appropriation
> in their personal lives, then that means that it is indeed possible to
> do so. Our existence can in a sense prove that the appropriation
> of women results from a social relationship and not a biological
> fact, that the category "women" is a social construct and not a
> natural group.

Since the term "lesbian" is often conflated with the term "feminist" (as in the case of anti-feminist events at Canadian universities) feminists are still required to illustrate that they are not lesbians. This requirement, then, is not so much a requirement to illustrate that you are not having sex with women, but that you are not *those other things that lesbians may be*; for example, more or less independent from men, directing energy towards women, not servicing men, and/or making men irrelevant. These activists pointed out that although the term "lesbian" when used in a regulatory manner is most often connected to "manhater," it is in fact more the refusal to do gender right, that is, to be a Woman, that is to be in the service of Men, that incurs this term:

> The other thing is you know, they think that lesbians trash men,
> and I don't, but I hear straight women trash them all the time.
> Because I am not invested in their life, they are not in my home,
> they are not major people in my life, they are certainly not my
> life partners, I have brothers that I love a lot but they are not a
> major part of my life . . . I like them for Sunday dinner and then I
> like them to go away. (activist 16)

> The myth about lesbians is that we hate men, I just don't see that
> many lesbians putting energy into hating men, I just think they
> are so irrelevant to our lives, and we don't take them that serious-
> ly and it's heterosexual women who have to live with them and

put up with them, that put a lot more energy into them, part of which is having to put up with them. (activist 12)

The leap from "lesbian" to "anti-men" was made quickly in the case of Hamilton's Sexual Assault Centre. The subsequent escalation of the controversy over the following months was, in part, a response to the Centre's refusal to step back into line, and its refusal to agree that the category "lesbian" was not one that should be associated with women's organizations. From the moment the Centre did not apologize for the inclusion of the category "lesbian," there were questions raised about its mandate. Very soon "lesbian" was conflated with "anti-male" as several ex-service users complained to the local councillors and local reporters who had been involved in the debate over the "lesbian ad." There were processes of discipline and punishment which eventually culminated in a full-scale review by the centre's three main funders. Although this review was ostensibly initiated as a response to lack of public confidence in the Centre, its origins can in fact be traced back to the "lesbian ad." This is not to suggest that women's complaints about service at the Centre were not justified, or that services at the Centre were not lacking. However, given that, (a) these complaints were only a handful out of more than three thousand women served annually by the centre,[10] and (b) presumably all organizations receive complaints, a full-scale, publicly discussed review appears to have been excessive.

There is certainly evidence in the final report of the review done by Avebury Research and Consulting (1993) that the "lesbian-bias" of the Centre was investigated extensively through the research process (Avebury Research and Consulting 1993: Appendix A). However, there is little discussion in the main body of the final report of the "lesbian-bias"; it remains unclear as to whether or not this accusation was substantiated in the widely thrown net of consultation. What this "demonization" of feminists and feminist organizations (as lesbian and anti-male) does do, in part, is regulate the kinds of activities which take place in and through these spaces of resistance. The accusations and/or criticisms of particular local feminists and/or organizations being anti-men, anti-police, too political and having a "lesbian bias" reached a wide audience through being played out in the media. The concrete consequences of UnWomanly Acts, such as organizational reviews, legal punishment, threatened loss of funding, loss of employment, and public vilification all send a message to other women's organizations in the same way that incidents of men's violence against females send a clear warning message to all women.

> Women are running scared right now, and it is frightening. And I think I have a lot to lose too, we all have a lot to lose. (activist 14)

The Centre was also heavily criticized by local councillors and in the review, for "anti-male" and "anti-police" attitudes (Hughes 1993). This activist described her experiences of the police in Hamilton:

> Women have been thrown into squad cars and arrested instead of their partners. Sorry I am sounding anti-police–that is the reality. The reason that people are anti-police is that the police have done something to make them anti-police. It's like saying "why are you anti-men?" "Oh, I don't know, I just thought it was a good idea!" (activist 5)

The point being, of course, that given that the police, for example, have been part of that system which has been identified by activists as perpetuating men's violence against females, there is a logic to those activists providing women with a realistic picture of what they *might* experience if they report to the police and go through the legal system. The processes operating here to discipline activists for being "anti-police" and/or "anti-male" (also read: lesbian) are similar to those which operate to disallow women's very justifiable (and totally logical) anger about men's violence against females. These discursive and political processes are part of the prescription to do gender right; which in this case is that Women must be nice, cooperative and conciliatory, in almost any context. In fact, the recommendations contained in the final report of the review of the Sexual Assault Centre concerning the centre's relationship with the police, the crown attorney's office and other local service organizations, are in essence about being more "balanced" and "co-ordinating," and that contact with the public should be "presented in such a way that the audience can 'hear' it" (Avebury Research and Consulting 1993: 40). Just like a well-behaved Woman. In particular the reviewers conclude that:

> The Centre's political activism has resulted in an increase in the community's knowledge about sexual violence against women

and in some positive attitudinal change. . . . Unfortunately this activism (although not always conducted as a Centre activity) has also strained the Centre's relationships with the police and the Crown's Attorney's office and has served to isolate the Centre from the justice system. (ibid. 40 & 41)

By positing that the proper mandate of the centre ought to include "getting along with" state institutions (rather than confronting them) the findings of the review reduce this space of political resistance from one that is *in and against* the state, to one that is most clearly simply *in* the state. Since continued funding was dependent upon the implementation of recommendations such as improving relations with the police and the crown attorney's office, the opportunity for action which would clearly *confront* these institutions is reduced. The prescription that the Sexual Assault Centre get along better with state institutions in the community constitutes, in part, the institutional level of the regulatory fiction of gender.

CONCLUSIONS

Structural change of the type imagined by early anti-violence activists has not been achieved. I have argued that the deradicalization of local anti-violence activism can be further understood as being the punitive consequences of activists not "doing gender right," individually, collectively and/or institutionally. "Lesbian," "man-hating" and "anti-police" were the most common regulatory terms used to contain this activism. However, instead of *building* on the clarity and potential afforded by those subjects radically located *in and against* the heterosexual regime, organized anti-violence activism has tended to marginalize it, silence it, and distance itself from those particular locations. Halton Women's Place apologized for the "lesbian ad," the Sexual Assault Centre and Justice For Women were criticized by other feminists. By accepting that individual activists and/or organizations should *not* be "lesbian," "anti-male" and "anti-police," "the movement" strengthens rather than weakens the oppressive boundaries of the category Woman. The power that the fiction of gender has to regulate the lives of females individually, collectively, and institutionally is shored up. As the concept of "good girls" and all of its manifestations are reproduced rather than contested, certain strategies for change are less punished than others. That is, activists argued that the second goal of "the movement" had been achieved; that is, strategies for providing safe and supportive services for women had been successful. I want to suggest that these strategies encounter less cultural and institutional opposition since they are most clearly within Women's mandate–listening, helping, caring, and servicing. In this way, then, activists are in fact "doing gender right."

In marginalizing UnWomanly praxis to illustrate that we are not threatening, we not only become just that–un-threatening–but we also *remove* those ideas and practices from the development of political identities in certain spaces of resistance. In this way the potential of these spaces to be "hotbeds" for the radicalization of females is effectively lost. This paper reveals concretely how the transformative potential of local feminist activism continues to be defused, in part, not only by the term lesbian but by the term Woman. By constructing and punishing certain types of UnWomanly Acts, regulatory bodies use discipline to force the proper doing of gender–thus stabilizing the fiction whilst simultaneously reducing the potential for these acts to reduce its regulatory power. This work adds voice to recent calls for an end to the "ongoing non-examination" of compulsory heterosexuality in geography and suggests the importance of a more widespread recognition in the discipline that the political regime of heterosexuality is as central to the construction of women's oppression as is racism, colonialism, classism, ableism, and sexism.

NOTES

1. The research draws on my own involvement in local political struggles and on interviews with 25 "white feminist anti-violence activists." I chose this group of women, in part, in order to investigate the differences *within* categories. That is, as organized feminism in Canada has begun to change in response to challenges from women who have been situated outside its largely white, middle-class, non-disabled and heterosexual subject, previously marginalized women have often been constructed as being "to blame" for the fragmentation of "the movement." This characterization implies the existence of a "unified" movement prior to these challenges, one which my experiences suggested did not exist. I was interested in critically exploring the implications of too much commonality having been presumed of an infrequently problematized group–"white feminists" (see Grant 1996).

2. The city of Hamilton is located at the heart of southern Ontario's industrial region, on the western edge of Lake Ontario. The municipality of over 300,000 inhabitants sits in the shadow of the much larger metropolitan conglomeration of To-

ronto, 70 kilometres around the lake (Statistics Canada 1992). Its emergence as a major industrial city at the centre of the Canadian steel production gave it its other name, Steel City (Dear et al. 1987). As has been the case with other industrial centres in North America, Hamilton's manufacturing industry has experienced the depressing effects of global economic restructuring. However, despite the reduction in the importance of the steel industry in the city's economy, it continues to play an influential role in the image of the city within Canada, and in the city's image of itself (Eyles and Peace 1990). The working class male subject is very much alive in the masculinist social, political and economic relations of a city known best for its hard hats, lunch buckets and a football team that likes to "eat them raw."

3. I use the term men's violence against females rather than the more common male violence against women for two main reasons: (1) to make explicit that in my conceptualization of it, men's violence is not a function of their maleness–but something that is manufactured; and (2) that all females, whether "women" or not, are seen as legitimate targets for this violence.

4. This is, of course, only one of many competing discourses on male violence against women. Dominant discourses, such as those manifested in relations of law, 'mental health,' the 'helping professions' and social services, compete with each other and with varied feminist discourses for legitimacy. What that set of variable discourses which can be broadly labelled feminist is competing with, is a set of discourses which continue to be informed by the "precipitation" myth–the notion that females are the cause of men's violence.

5. Lesbians hardly appear in Gillian Walker's otherwise impressive analysis of the "conceptual politics of struggle" between the anti-violence movement and the Ontario state (Walker 1990); they appear infrequently (outside of the discussion of lesbian abuse) in *Listening to the Thunder: advocates talk about the battered women's movement*, the recent collection of 20 articles put together by the Vancouver Women's Research Centre (Timmins 1995); and, Dobash and Dobash (1992), in their analysis of the movements in Britain and the United States, understand lesbian existence as something private and not directly connected to the issue (see especially pp. 55).

6. The activists are identified by number alone. I realize this is not the most satisfactory form of identification; however, the "community" is small enough that descriptions such as "shelter worker, lesbian, mid-40s" would threaten the promised confidentiality. Activists were numbered quite simply, that is, in order of being interviewed.

7. A card attached to each rose stated, "We demand justice for Debra Ellul. Debra Ellul was murdered on February 5, 1989. Guy Ellul was acquitted of all charges December 6, 1990. Debra Ellul was stabbed by Guy Ellul 21 times. Sponsored by the Justice For Women Coalition."

8. "Women Protest Injustice." Justice For Women flyer (n.d.).

9. The editorial complained: "Lobbyists are everywhere. Walk through the corridors of power–whether it be at Parliament buildings, Queen's Park or city hall–and it is impossible not to run into someone who is grinding an axe for some group" (Hamilton Spectator 1992: A8).

10. The Centre was informed of, but never shown, eleven anonymous complaints which had been made to a local councillor and to members of the local media.

REFERENCES

Avebury Research and Consulting (1993) Independent Client Service Review of the Sexual Assault Centre (Hamilton and Area) (Avebury Research and Consulting Ltd., Toronto).

Bell, David, Jon Binnie, Julia Cream and Gill Valentine (1994) 'All Hyped Up and No Place To Go', *Gender, Place and Culture: a journal of feminist geography* 1, pp. 31-47.

Bell, David and Gill Valentine (1995a) (eds.) *Mapping Desire: geographies of sexualities* (Routledge, London).

Bell, David and Gill Valentine (1995b) 'The Sexed Self: strategies of performance, sites of resistance', in Pile, Steve and Nigel Thrift (eds.) *Mapping the Subject: geographies of cultural transformation* (Routledge, London and New York) pp. 143-157.

Black, Debra (1991) 'Fighting Back On Campus', *The Toronto Star* December 2, pp. C1 and C3.

Brown, Barbara (1992a) 'Slain woman's mother pledges there'll be justice for Debra', *The Spectator* January 23, pp. A1.

——— (1992b) "To hell with politics", *The Spectator* August 4, pp. A1.

Butler, Judith (1990) *Gender Trouble: feminism and the subversion of identity* (Routledge, London and New York).

Casella, Emilia (1992) "'No reason' for Ellul inquiry Justice for Debra Coalition told', *The Spectator* November 10, pp. B1.

Chouinard, Vera and Ali Grant (1995) 'On Being Not Even Anywhere Near 'The Project': Ways of Putting Ourselves In The Picture', *Antipode* 27, pp. 137-166.

Cream, Julia (1995) 'Re-Solving Riddles: the sexed body', in David Bell and Gill Valentine (eds.) *Mapping Desire: geographies of sexualities* (Routledge, London) pp. 31-40.

Davy, Denise (1992a) "Victims protest court 'injustice'", *The Spectator* July 28, pp. C1.

——— (1992b) 'Pull crown off wife assault cases: coalition', *The Spectator* August 15, pp. B1.

Dear, M.J., J.J. Drake and L.G. Reeds (1987) (eds.) *Steel City. Hamilton and Region* (University of Toronto Press, Toronto).

Deverell, Johan (1992) "Women protest 'travesty of justice'", *The Toronto Star* November 10, pp. A10.

Dobash, R.E. and Dobash, R.P (1992) *Women, Violence and Social Change* (Routledge, New York).

Duncan, Nancy (1996) (ed.) *BodySpace: destabilizing geographies of gender and sexuality* (Routledge, London).

Durocher, Constance (1990) 'Heterosexuality: Sexuality or Social System?', *Resources for Feminist Research* 19, 3/4 pp. 13-18.

Eyles, John and Walter Peace (1990) 'Signs and Symbols in Hamilton: An Iconology of Steeltown', *Geografiska Annaler* 72B, 2-3 pp. 73-88.

Frye, Marilyn (1983) *The Politics of Reality: Essays in Feminist Theory* (The Crossing Press, New York).

_____ (1992) *Willful Virgin: Essays in Feminism 1976-1992* (The Crossing Press, Freedom CA).

Gibson-Graham, J.K (1994) "'Stuffed If I Know!': reflections on post-modern feminist social research", *Gender, Place and Culture: a journal of feminist geography* 1, 2 pp. 205-224.

Grant, Ali (1996) *Geographies of Oppression and Resistance: Contesting the Reproduction of the Heterosexual Regime* Unpublished PhD Thesis (McMaster University, Hamilton).

_____ (forthcoming) 'Dyke Geographies: All Over The Place', in Griffin, Gabriele and Sonya Andermahr (eds.) *Straight Studies Modified: Lesbian Interventions in the Academy* (Cassell).

Harris, Debbie Wise (1989) 'Keeping Women In Our Place: Violence At Canadian Universities', *Canadian Woman Studies* 11, 4 pp. 37-41.

Hamilton Spectator (1991) 'Assault centre head charged in paint attack', *The Spectator* December 5.

_____ (1992) 'Editorial: a wider vision', *The Spectator* September 2, pp. A8.

Holt, Jim (1991) 'To Serve and Protect' *The Spectator* November 30, pp. A1 & D1.

Hughes, Rick (1993) 'More assault centre complaints', *The Spectator* February 4, pp. D3.

Johnson, Louise (1994) 'What future for feminist geography?', *Gender, Place and Culture: a journal of feminist geography* 2, pp. 103-113.

Justice For Women (1992) 'Group Launches Continuing Protest Against Ellul Decision', *Justice For Women Coalition News Release* January 24.

Keith, Michael and Steve Pile (1993) (eds.) *Place and the Politics of Identity* (Routledge, London and New York).

Knopp, Larry (1995) 'If You're Going To Get All Hyped Up You'd Better Go Somewhere!', *Gender, Place and Culture: a journal of feminist geography* 2, pp. 85-88.

Kobayashi, Audrey and Linda Peake (1994) 'Unnatural Discourse. 'Race' and Gender in Geography', *Gender, Place and Culture: a journal of feminist geography* 1, 2 pp. 225-244.

Lefaive, Doug (1992a) 'Spray-paint fine too harsh women say' *The Spectator* February 21, pp. B1.

_____ (1992b) 'Review clears Crown lawyer's return to domestic assault cases', *The Spectator* August 28, pp. B1.

Longbottom, Ross (1992) '$500,000 promise survives controversial 'lesbian' ad', *The Spectator* November 27, pp. B4.

Longhurst, Robyn (1995) 'The Body and Geography', *Gender, Place and Culture: a journal of feminist geography* 2, 1 pp. 97-105.

Marlin, Beth (1991) 'Courts, police protected cop group charges', *The Spectator* December 3, pp. A1.

McDowell, Linda and Gill Court (1994) 'Performing work: bodily representations in merchant banks', *Environment and Planning D: Society and Space* 12, pp. 727-750.

Nicholson, Linda (1990) (ed.) *Feminism/Postmodernism* (Routledge, New York).

Peake, Linda (1993) "'Race' and sexuality: challenging the patriarchal structuring of urban social space", Environment and Planning D: Society and Space 11 pp. 415-432.

Peters, Ken (1993a) "'Lesbian' job ad draws political fire", *The Spectator* January 12, pp. B1.

⸺ (1993b) "'Ignorance' behind debate over lesbian ad", *The Spectator* January 13, pp. B1.

Pierson, Ruth Roach (1990) 'Violence Against Women: Strategies for Change' *Canadian Woman Studies* 11, 4 pp. 10-12.

Pile, Steve and Nigel Thrift (1995) (eds.) *Mapping the Subject: geographies of cultural transformation* (Routledge, London and New York).

Pratt, Geraldine and Susan Hanson (1994) 'Geography and the Construction of Difference', *Gender, Place and Culture: a journal of feminist geography* 1, 1 pp. 5-29.

Probyn, Elspeth (1995) 'Lesbians In Space. Gender, Sex and the Structure of Missing', *Gender, Place and Culture: a journal of feminist geography* 2 pp. 77-84.

Prokaska, Lee (1993a) 'Justice vigil into 2nd year', *The Spectator* January 27, pp. B1.

⸺ (1993b) 'Her quest for Debra', *The Spectator* January 28, pp. D2.

Rose, Gillian (1993) *Feminism & Geography: The Limits of Geographical Knowledge* (University of Minnesota Press, Minneapolis).

Statistics Canada (1992) *Profile of census tracts in Hamilton, Part A* (Industry, Science and Technology Canada, Ottawa), 1991 Census of Canada. Catalogue Number 95-341.

Tait, Eleanor (1992) "'Lesbian' ad jeopardizes funds for women's shelter", *The Spectator* November 20, pp. B6.

Timmins, Leslie (1995) (ed.) *Listening to the Thunder: Advocates Talk About The Battered Women's Movement* (Women's Research Centre, Vancouver).

Tyler, Tracey (1992) 'Appeal ruled out in slaying acquittal', *The Toronto Star* January 23.

Valentine, Gill (1993a) 'Desperately seeking Susan: a geography of lesbian friendships' *Area* 25 pp. 109-116.

⸺ (1993b) 'Negotiating and managing multiple sexual identities: lesbian time-space strategies', *Transactions, Institute of British Geographers NS* 18 pp. 237-248.

⸺ (1993c) '(Hetero)sexing space: lesbian perceptions and experiences of everyday space', *Environment and Planning D: Society and Space* 11 pp. 395-413.

Walker, Gillian A (1990) *Family Violence and the Women's Movement: The Conceptual Politics of Struggle* (University of Toronto Press, Toronto).

Wittig, Monique (1992) *The Straight Mind and other essays* (Beacon Press, Boston).

"Sticks and Stones May Break My Bones": A Personal Geography of Harassment

Gill Valentine

WRITING PERSONAL GEOGRAPHIES

The authority of personal experience was a central tenet of 1970s British and North American feminism, epitomised by the mantra of the time: "the personal is political." It produced a significant amount of personal testimony in the social sciences, although feminist geographers have until recently been notably more circumspect about baring their souls in academic writing than have feminist writers in sociology and anthropology or those in literary and cultural criticism, where there is a tradition of this form of writing (exceptions include, for example, Chouinard and Grant, 1995; personal testimonies from a number of women geographers in the Women and Geography Study Group, 1997; Bondi, 1997; Moss, 1998). Indeed, in the late 1980s and early 1990s, under the influence of postmodernist/poststructuralist strands of thought, the disciplines of both sociology and anthropology have been marked by increased critical attention to biography and autobiographical forms of writing as both methodological sources and as "methodologies" in themselves (see, for example, Stanley, 1992; Okely and Callaway, 1992).

Within Geography, issues of self-reflexivity have hinged less on

Gill Valentine is Professor of Human Geography at the University of Sheffield, Sheffield, England (e-mail: G.Valentine@sheffield.ac.uk).

This essay originally appeared in *Antipode* 30: 4, 1998, pp. 305-332 (Blackwell Publishers, 350 Main Street, Malden, MA 02148). Reprinted by permission.

[Haworth co-indexing entry note]: "'Sticks and Stones May Break My Bones": A Personal Geography of Harassment." Valentine, Gill. Co-published simultaneously in *Journal of Lesbian Studies* (Harrington Park Press, an imprint of The Haworth Press, Inc.) Vol. 4, No. 1, 2000, pp. 81-112; and: *From Nowhere to Everywhere: Lesbian Geographies* (ed: Gill Valentine) Harrington Park Press, an imprint of The Haworth Press, Inc., 2000, pp. 81-112.

questions of autobiographical writing and more on the significance of the researcher's identity and position in the research process (see, for example, McDowell, 1992; Katz, 1992). Critical geographers (including feminists, postcolonial writers, poststructuralists, and so on) have challenged the false neutrality of much work within the discipline, arguing that "all knowledge is produced in specific circumstances and that those circumstances shape it in some way" (Rose, 1997:305). As a result, the claim that by reflexively examining our own positionality in our research and research relationships and writing this into our own work we can make more explicit the embodied and situated nature of our knowledges has become a familiar refrain in a growing number of special issues or collections within geographical journals (see, for example, *Environment and Planning D: Society and Space*, Volume 10 [1992]; *The Professional Geographer*, Volume 46 [1994]; *Antipode*, Volume 27 [1995]). In a review of this literature, Rose (1997:311) critiques much of the soul-searching about the nature of power relations embedded in research practices by pointing out the "impossibility of such a quest to know fully both self and context." Instead, she draws upon Butler's (1990) book *Gender Trouble*, in which Butler famously maintains that identities do not preexist our performances and thus are profoundly unstable, arguing that because identities are relational (that is, they exist through mutually constitutive social relations), then consequently research is constitutive both of the researcher and others involved in the research process. Rose (1997:316) writes that "researcher, researched and research make each other; research and selves [are] 'interactive texts.'" It is a process, she argues, that is complex, uncertain, incomplete, and saturated with power.

Reading Rose's paper stirred in me a latent realisation of how much of my own identity has been made and remade through my own research, writing, and encounter with the discipline of Geography. While I recognise the difficulties of self-reflection that are neatly expressed by Gibson-Graham (1994:206) when she argues that she is not a knowing and centred subject but rather is "un-centred, un-certain, not entirely present, not fully representable," at the same time Rose's paper made me think about how absent I am from my own research and writing (even my acknowledgements often seem more impersonal, more falsely neutral than many others I read) and yet how much my sexual identity, geographical research, and identity as an academic have been mutually constitutive of each other.

Although the choice of geographies of sexualities (for example, Valentine, 1993a) as a research topic at the beginning of my academic career was largely motivated by my own personal experiences, most notably as a lesbian, I never set out to "come out" within the discipline. While my sexual identity was constituting my research, I never intended this relationship to be mutual. Indeed, I rather naively believed that I could walk a tightrope of ambiguity within Geography about my own sexuality, while still writing about lesbian geographies. In doing so, I forgot that texts can exceed or escape authorial intentions–in this case with the consequence that the discipline somewhat thrust the identity "lesbian-geographer" upon me, prefacing my previously unhyphenated, asexual academic identity with a sexual signifier. If this had happened a decade or more earlier, I would undoubtedly never have made it past go in the profession. Yet, thanks to a combination of the efforts of feminist geographers[1] in the late 1970s and early 1980s to establish a bridgehead both for women geographers and for feminist thought within the discipline and of the more recent postmodernism-inspired concern with "difference" and the neglected voice of "the other" that has permeated most areas of human geography in the 1990s, I have found an intellectual and social space within the discipline among what can loosely be called "critical geographies/ers."

On the one hand, then, the mutual constitution of my sexual, research, and academic identities has been a positive, welcome, and often very supportive experience. Yet, on the other hand, this process has fixed my academic identity around my sexual identity in a way that I sometimes find imprisoning and unhelpful. Even though I have tried to perform my academic identity differently through my subsequent research–writing about children, parenting, food, and most recently prison, masculinity, and disability–I have not been able to destabilise the certainty with which my early research has constituted my identity as a lesbian-geographer.[2]

I have sometimes felt uncomfortable about this; it has placed me in a rather paradoxical position, for while I have been held up as a "lesbian-geographer" who is assumed to be "out" both publicly and privately, I have actually been performing a very different identity to my family, creating a very precarious "public"/"private," "work"/ "home" splintered existence. To add to the irony, it was, of course, writing about how other women manage just such multiple subjectivities that has helped to create and therefore exacerbate the cleavages in my own life (see, for example, Valentine, 1993a, 1993b, 1993c, 1996a).

None of this has really mattered that much–until now, that is. The reason Rose's (1997) paper about the mutual constitution of research-researcher-researched had such a personal impact upon me was because at the time of reading it (and indeed at the time of writing this) I had been receiving hate mail, much of which, though not all, has referred to my sexual identity, my research, my teaching, and my position within the discipline of Geography.

What follows is an account of my experience of receiving malicious homophobic mail and silent phone calls, having a distorted threatening voice recorded onto my answer machine, and being "outed" to my parents. It is a paper about the geography of harassment in which I revisit "the geographies" that I have written about before as a semidetached observer, for which I have "borrowed" others' accounts of fear, sexual violence, "coming-out" narratives, lesbian identity, and "power" (for example, Valentine, 1989, 1993a), but this time I explore them as they are refracted through the lens of my own personal geography. At the same time, because "Geography" is the institutional framework for my experiences of harassment and because these experiences are bound up with my place in the discipline and have to a certain extent remade my "identity" by enmeshing me in the contradictions of my own life, it is also very much about the mutual constitution of my sexual identity, my "family" identity, my academic identity, my research, and the discipline. Of course, as thoughts are being put to paper, words have a habit of pinning meanings down, making the complex simple and the uncertain fixed–personal writing in particular tends to imply a unity of the self. While I am aware of this and I want to try to avoid doing so, I will undoubtedly fall into this trap at some point.

Stanley (1992:246), in discussing autobiographical writing, has argued that *bio*, the narration of the material events of everyday life, is the crucial element in the theorising and understanding both of *auto* ("self") and *graph* ("writing"). So I want to begin by outlining a particular set of material events that are the main point of reference for all that follows. Having established this narrative (which, of course, is only one account out of many possible ways I could have told the story), I want to go on to interpret this experience by exploring a number of themes: first, to describe the different processes (all of which play upon the mutual constitution of my academic self and sexual self) through which my harasser has sought to exclude me from the discipline of Geography; second, to think about the geography of harassment–about how hate mail and silent calls can disrupt meanings of place, particularly the way that personal geographies can be taken for granted until they are transgressed; third, to examine geographies of the law; and, finally, to return to where I began this paper, by considering the mutual constitution of research–self–geography.

THE EVENTS

My story begins in the summer of 1997, when I began to be plagued by silent phone calls, the caller using the cloak of anonymity afforded by British Telecom's recently introduced "caller withheld number" facility. Initially, always in the daytime, the calls took the form both of "silences" recorded onto my answer machine at home and of hang-up calls at home and (less frequently) at work.

Then, in the autumn, my phantom caller switched tactics, first targeting me with silent calls in the evening, then escalating the harassment still further with calls in the middle of the night and early hours of the morning. Beginning to feel the effects of sleep deprivation, at this point I rang the British Telecom Nuisance Caller Bureau to investigate what action could be taken. The woman I spoke to offered to change my phone number, but as my number was not in the directory anyway, I knew that the caller must be someone embedded into my own social networks, someone who would have little trouble finding out a new number, so there seemed no point in pursuing this offer. I opted instead to tell as many friends and acquaintances as possible that I was investigating the possibility of putting a trace on my line. Five months after they had begun, the calls stopped. It was Christmas and I thought no more about it.

Early in January I stumbled through my door, exhausted, having driven back to Sheffield nonstop from Cornwall, where I had spent a long weekend celebrating my birthday. I collected my mail, slumped into a chair, picked up the phone to call a friend, and with the receiver jammed between my shoulder and chin began opening my birthday mail. I was in mid-sentence when suddenly I went silent and just said,

"Oh my God." In an envelope that had been addressed to me but posted to my parents' home and then forwarded unopened to my home in Sheffield was a white piece of paper with letters cut out of newspaper headlines, spelling out the message, "I'm going to tell your family you're a sick dyke pig" (Figure 1).

I called the police. To date it has proved to be the first of nine letters.[3] Some, like the one below, are short messages cut out of letters from newspaper headlines, while others are long typed diatribes. They have been posted from six different locations in the United Kingdom and sent to my parents' address, my home address, and my department. Each has taken a different theme; these include my sexual orientation, my personal relationships, my research, my teaching, and my postgraduate supervision, and some have insisted that I "quit" Geography and have threatened to "out" me to my family. The contents suggest that the perpetrator is a member of the discipline of Geography who is closely linked to my professional networks. Some imply that the sender is an individual, others that the sender is part of a network dedicated to "purifying" the academy. They have been accompanied by the return of sporadic silent nighttime calls, the recording of a distorted threatening voice on my answer machine, and the ringing of my doorbell in the middle of the night.

Just before I left for the 1998 Association of American Geographers (AAG) Annual Conference, I received a letter that ended with the veiled threat, "One guess where the next letter is headed for" (Figure 2). When

FIGURE 1. Letter 1

I returned to work from the conference, another letter was waiting for me; this time it read, "Scum . . . fucker[,] they know! Quit[,] slack cunt" (Figure 3). And, sure enough, my harasser had indeed carried out the threat to out me to my parents by sending them a list of my publications on lesbian geographies, with accompanying unpleasantries.[4] I hoped that this might sate my harasser's appetite for spite and maliciousness, but at the time of writing this I am still receiving abusive mail.

PROCESSES OF EXCLUSION: GEOGRAPHY'S BOUNDARIES AND CONNECTIONS

In *Geographies of Exclusion*, Sibley (1995) draws on psychoanalytical and social-anthropological writings to explore the construction of self and other and the way in which these identities are connected to

FIGURE 2. Letter 4

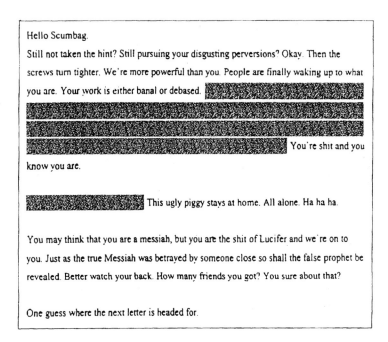

Hello Scumbag.

Still not taken the hint? Still pursuing your disgusting perversions? Okay. Then the screws turn tighter. We're more powerful than you. People are finally waking up to what you are. Your work is either banal or debased. ███████████ ██ ██ ██████████████████████ You're shit and you know you are.

████████████ This ugly piggy stays at home. All alone. Ha ha ha.

You may think that you are a messiah, but you are the shit of Lucifer and we're on to you. Just as the true Messiah was betrayed by someone close so shall the false prophet be revealed. Better watch your back. How many friends you got? You sure about that?

One guess where the next letter is headed for.

Edited to remove personal references to other people.

FIGURE 3. Letter 6

Edited to remove personal references to other people.

social, material, and cultural contexts. In particular, he harnesses Kristeva's concept of abjection to think about boundaries between self and other. In her essay on abjection, Kristeva suggests that the subject feels a sense of repulsion at its own residues (excrement, decay, infection, etc.), which "stand for the danger to identity that comes from without: the ego threatened by the non-ego, society threatened by its outside, life by death" (Kristeva, 1982: 71, quoted in Sibley, 1995:8). To maintain the purity of the self, the boundaries of the body must be constantly defended in a never-ending battle against the impure. Sibley (1995:8) argues that "the urge to make separations between clean and dirty, ordered and disordered, 'us' and 'them,' that is to expel the abject, is encouraged in western cultures, creating feelings of anxiety because such separations can never be achieved." Sibley (1995:14) goes on:

> The determination of a border between the inside and the outside according to the simple logic of "excluding filth," as Kristeva puts it, or the imperative of "distancing from disgust" (Constance Perin) translates into several different corporeal or social images which signal imperfection or a low ranking in a hierarchy of being. Exclusionary discourse draws particularly on colour, disease, animals, sexuality and nature, but they all come back to the idea of dirt as a signifier of imperfection and inferiority.

This consistent imagery of defilement is evident in the fifth malicious letter I received (Figure 4). All the exclusionary discourses cited by Sibley, with the exception of colour, are mobilised in the writer's quest to "purify" the academy (my emphasis in boldface, harasser's emphasis underlined):

> We know about you and your little lesbo "friends," all about you. You are sinners, the lot of you. We've watched you manipulate your way into our ranks and its [sic] time now that someone puts a stop to it. We held court and decided you are the worst of a **diseased, sick breed** of **deviants**. You are a **pollution**. . . . You are **rabid**, beyond redemption and evil. You know now that we have networks. [Prof. X] may have brown-nosed the VC [vice chancellor] on your behalf but some of us here were delighted to get rid of you. People everywhere know you are **sick** and you are so despised that its [sic] not difficult to find people to give us information about you. We have associates in all places, including Sheffield, and we have information about you, your **disgusting** behaviour and your **dirty** little "friends." We know your movements and we're going to bring you down. Your **repugnant** behaviour has to be exposed for your own salvation. We'll no longer let the likes of you **corrupt** and **pollute** academia. We consider it our purpose to blow your little networks apart and drive the lot of you out. Take our advice and get lost.

Disease and filth, which appear in Letter 5 and are also freely employed in Letters 1, 2, and 9 (Figures 1, 5, and 9, respectively), are

FIGURE 4. Letter 5

```
We know about you and your little lesbo 'friends', all about
you. You are sinners, the lot of you. We've watched you
manipulate your way into our ranks and its time now that
someone puts a stop to it. We held court and decided you are
the worst of a diseased, sick breed of deviants. You are a
pollution ███████████████████████. You are rabid, beyond
redemption and evil. You know now that we have networks.
█████████ may have brown-nosed the VC on your behalf but
some of us here were delighted to get rid of you. People
everywhere know you are sick and you are so despised that
its not difficult to find people to give us information
about you. We have associates in all places, including
Sheffield, and we have information about you, your
disgusting behaviour and your dirty little 'friends'. We
know your movements and we're going to bring you down. Your
repugnant behaviour has to be exposed for your own
salvation. We'll no longer let the likes of you corrupt and
pollute academia. We consider it our purpose to blow your
little networks apart and drive the lot of you out. Take our
advice and get lost.
```

Edited to remove personal references to other people.

particularly potent negative stereotypes because not only do they represent a mark of imperfection, but they also carry a threat of contagion. The "diseased other" threatens the "normal" majority with infection and ultimately collapse. This imagery is most evident in relation to contemporary moral panics about sexual dissidents and AIDS (Sibley, 1995).

Letters 3 (Figure 6) and 6 (Figure 3) take a different approach, using imagery of stigmatised forms of sexuality to signify my imperfection and inferiority–images that are contradictory in that they are mutually exclusive. For while on the one hand Letter 3 opts for the accusation that I am a "frigid dyke," Letter 6 draws on an oppositional stereotype–"slack cunt."

References to animals and nature (breed, rabid) feature in Letter 5 (cited above) and more explicitly in Letters 1, 3, 7, and 8 (Figures 1, 6, 7, and 8, respectively), where I am referred to as a pig, a cow, and a slug. Sibley (1995) points out that animals are abject–in the sense that animals are represented as inferior to humans (savage, uncivilised), but also in the way that particular species, for example, pigs or rats, are associated with residues (such as waste, sewage). This is most visibly evident in this excerpt from Letter 7 (Figure 7), written right after the

FIGURE 5. Letter 2

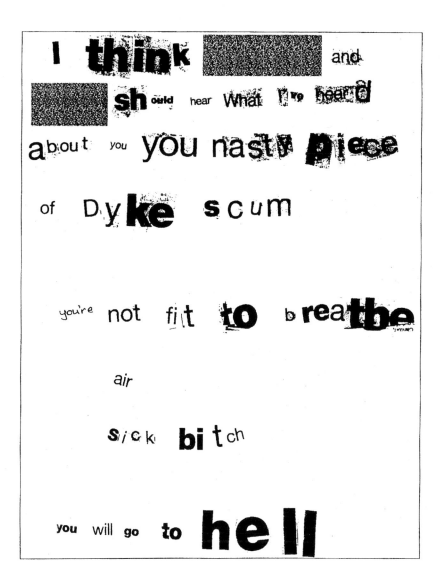

Edited to remove personal references to other people.

FIGURE 6. Letter 3

GILL VALENTINE:

STROPPY, MOODY, SELF-CENTRED, CAREERIST COW.

THIS IS WHAT YOUR COLLEAGUES AND STUDENTS AND EVERYONE ELSE YOU HAVEN'T CONNED THINK OF YOU. NASTY, UGLY, PRICK-TEASING, FRIGID DYKE.

WONDER WHAT YOUR PARENTS THINK OF THEIR LITTLE DARLING? DO THEY KNOW WHAT THEY ARE RESPONSIBLE FOR? THEY SHOULD.

AAG conference in March: "We saw you, by the way. Or rather we **smelled** you as you walked past. You look like a **pig** and you **smell like a pig**. One day we'll get rid of the **stench**. In the meantime, we're watching you. Its [sic] still not too late to repent and stop pushing your **filth** down our throats" (my emphasis in bold). By employing a range of stereotypes and images that have important currency in western cultures in this way, the letters mobilise exclusionary discourses with the intent of driving me out of the discipline of Geography. In doing so, they implicitly represent Geography as a heterosexual space where I, as a lesbian, am not welcome.

Certainly, Geography has a well-documented masculinist, heterosexist, ableist, and colonial heritage (McDowell, 1990; Bell, 1991; Rose, 1993; Chouinard and Grant, 1995; Binnie, 1997). Although there are a significant number of sexual dissidents within the discipline (see Bell, 1994), Grant (1997) points out the conundrum of what she calls the "missing lesbians" or the "not-quite-as-visible-as-we-might-be lesbians" in the profession. This invisibility of lesbian-geographers, despite an academic climate in which more situated, embodied geographies are in vogue, is perhaps explained by Johnson (1994:110), who, writing on her own anxieties about coming out in the profession, explains, "I've agonised for years about the consequences–professional and otherwise–of 'coming out' in print, declaring my

FIGURE 7. Letter 7

```
Oh dear. We have been a naughty girl, haven't we? Its
amazing what people will tell you over a pint in a bar
at a conference. Even your little lesbo 'friends' know
what you are. And we know who they are, which makes
this all the more entertaining. You have made it so
easy for us. Its quite hilarious. We saw you, by the
way. Or rather we smelled you as you walked past. You
look like a pig and you smell like a pig. One day
we'll get rid of the stench. In the meantime, we're
watching you. Its still not too late to repent and
stop pushing your filth down our throats.
```

FIGURE 8. Letter 8

CHIEF CHEER-LEADER OF THE DIKE
CAUCUS? CHIEF SLIME-BAG MORE
LIKE. HALF OF THAT BUNCH OF UGLY
DEVIANTS THINKS SO TOO

EVER POURED SALT ON A SLUG?

STAY OUT OF THE SEA THIS SUMMER

own sexuality and building a feminist geography upon my lesbianism.
And basically I've seen the risks as too great, the stakes as too high in
a homophobic culture and discipline."

During my own career I have experienced a number of minor epi-
sodes of homophobia, including having my research on lesbian geographies left off a departmental research display, having my research
lambasted in the *News of the World* as a waste of taxpayers' money,
learning that an assessor from another department in an internal uni-

versity audit had suggested that my papers on lesbian geographies should not be included in the Research Assessment Exercise because of the subject matter, and being told that a geographer was alleged to have attempted to use my sexuality as grounds for opposing my appointment to that department.[5] On each occasion, colleagues both from within the departments concerned and from within "critical geography" have been supportive–and in some cases more horrified than I have been.

Despite a recognition of the heritage that underpins Geography and my knowledge (and experience) that sexism, homophobia, racism, and ableism permeate many departments, I do not feel excluded from Geography (or at least the parts of it that interest or matter to me).[6] Indeed, as I implied in the introduction to this paper, I feel positively embraced into particular areas of it. When I have received this hate mail, I have not therefore read it as an expression of a heterosexual discipline trying to purify itself, which is how I think the author intended me to read it–because to do so would be to fly in the face of my lived experiences. Rather, because the content of the letters suggests that the sender is closely linked to my professional networks, I have read them as the work of a critical geographer appropriating discourses of homophobia in order to try to force me out of the discipline for personal motives.

But even if the letters are only from one particular individual rather than, as they imply, from geographers as a whole or an organised group of geographers, how do I begin to defend the boundaries of my self, to locate and distance myself from the source of my defilement when I cannot contain or control the information that my harasser has about me? Several of the malicious letters contain information about my life that I believe should be known only to a handful of people (and that I have edited out of the material reproduced in this paper). As McNay (1994:27) writes, "Knowledge is not a form of pure speculation belonging to an abstract and disinterested realm of enquiry; rather it is at once a product of power relations and instrumental in sustaining these relations." In particular, the knowledge about my life being reproduced in the malicious letters is a product of academic networks in which all the geographers circulating within the discourses of e-mail threads, conference bar talk, and personal friendships are undergoing and exercising power through "talk." As the excerpts from Letters 4, 5, and 7 (Figures 2, 4, and 7, respectively) imply, through these networks I am under constant surveillance from an unseen observer:

> You may think that you are a messiah, but you are the shit of Lucifer and we're on to you. Just as the true Messiah was betrayed by someone close so shall the false prophet be revealed. Better watch your back. How many friends [have] you got? You sure about that? (Letter 4)

> ... you are so despised that its [sic] not difficult to find people to give us information about you. We have associates in all places, including Sheffield, and we have information about you, your disgusting behaviour and your dirty little "friends." We know your movements and we're going to bring you down. (Letter 5)

> Its [sic] amazing what people will tell you over a pint in a bar at a conference. Even your little lesbo "friends" know what you are. And we know who they are, which makes this all the more entertaining. You have made it so easy for us. Its [sic] quite hilarious. (Letter 7)

In turn, in a classic Foucauldian sense I am exercising self-surveillance–being vigilant about what, if anything, I say to whom, circumspect with my friends within the discipline about what I am doing, where I am going, about my teaching, my work, my students, my relationships, my family, and so on. I am at once excluding myself from professional networks, unable to connect with other geographers who have supported and sustained me within my job, yet at the same time I am still helpless to sever all the connections between myself and my persecutor. The self-contained and self-referential nature of any academic discipline means that, unlike in many others' careers where moving jobs can mark a fairly complete break with the past, where you leave your successes and mistakes behind you like a dead skin, within Geography it is impossible to shake off your own history. I have left a trail of information about myself stretched out behind me that I am helpless to reclaim. And so my harasser is free to pick over my past, to utilise the density of geographical social networks to find out not only about my present life but also my past connections with particular places and departments. As this extract from Letter 9 (Figure 9) indicates, this includes obtaining copies of my application forms:

FIGURE 9. Letter 9

I have some of your application forms in front of me.
They have just about done the rounds now.
People try to stop these things getting around, but they are actually very easy to get hold of.
They are also very interesting. Extremely nauseating, but very interesting.
It would all be quite amusing if it weren't so sick. Just the other day a few of us were chatting
about what most sickens us about you. One person, who met you for the first time in
Scotland recently, put his finger on it when he said his first thought on seeing you was "who
the fuck does she think she is?" Yes, it's your arrogance that we find so galling. You seem to
think that the shite you turn out is worthy. You are just a debased fucker, and the sooner you
realise that the better for all of us.
Has anyone told you about the web page? We just about have enough material now. It
should be a scream. It will also show the world what you really are – a sick menace who
shouldn't be allowed anywhere near kids. We'll be sending the address out soon. Don't
worry, the fall from the cess pool you dwell in won't be too hard.

I have some of your application forms in front of me. They have
just about done the rounds now. People try to stop these things
getting around, but they are actually very easy to get hold of.
They are also very interesting. Extremely nauseating, but very
interesting. It would all be quite amusing if it weren't so sick.

Indeed, my harasser's repertoire of intimidation has played upon the
geography of my work life, posting the letters from places where I
have previously worked or places associated in other ways with my
career, in what I assume is an attempt to use "place" to falsely impli-
cate as the sender(s) of the letters two geographers with whom I have
had strained working relationships.[7]

The more isolated and the more marginalised I have become from
my networks, the more fragile my belief in my own ability to produce
or perform the identity of competent academic has become. Despite
the old adage that "sticks and stones may break my bones, but names
will never hurt me," under the sort of barrage of criticism outlined in
the following extracts from Letters 3, 4, and 9 (Figures 6, 2, and 9,
respectively), I have found myself engaged in a constant introspective
search either for evidence that the accusations might be right or for
proof to convince myself that they are wrong:

GILL VALENTINE:
STROPPY, MOODY, SELF-CENTRED, CAREERIST COW.
THIS IS WHAT YOUR COLLEAGUES AND STUDENTS
AND EVERYONE ELSE YOU HAVEN'T CONNED THINK
OF YOU. NASTY, UGLY, PRICK-TEASING, FRIGID DYKE.
(Letter 3)

Hello[,] Scumbag.
Still not taken the hint? Still pursuing your disgusting perversions? Okay. Then the screws turn tighter. We're more powerful than you. People are finally waking up to what you are. Your work is either banal or debased. . . . You're shit and you know you are. (Letter 4)

Yes, it's your arrogance that we find so galling. You seem to think that the shite [sic] you turn out is worthy. You are just a debased fucker, and the sooner you realise that the better for all of us. (Letter 9)

As I have struggled to come to grips with this harassment and how to deal with it, I have felt my confidence as an academic seep away, impairing my concentration, blunting my ability to write, and undermining my willingness to attend conferences where I know that not only will I have to publicly perform my rather unstable identity as a "competent academic," but where I also know that my path will undoubtedly cross that of my harasser.[8]

These experiences have left me in a paradoxical space. On the one hand, I am being distanced from Geography/ers through three exclusionary processes. First, negative imagery is being used in the letters to delineate a boundary between Geography/ers and myself as the other. Second, the letters have forced me to withdraw from geographical networks in order to prevent my harasser mining information about my life from colleagues and academic friends. Third, by rupturing my self-confidence, the letters have eroded my visibility in the discipline by abbreviating my conference appearances and interfering with my ability to write. On the other hand, the letters have strengthened and deepened my connections with those geographers in whom I have confided about the harassment. They have prompted me to make an effort to repair one or two academic relationships that have been strained by particular events. They have motivated me to break out of my rather ghettoised existence in Geography by developing academic and social networks across other disciplines. They have made me more self-reflexive about my teaching: this year I received from students the highest teaching assessment scores of my career. And they have inspired me to return to writing about sexuality again–specifically inspiring me to apply for an Economic Social and Research Council grant on lesbian and gay youth. In this way, paradoxically, the more my harasser has tried to construct me as outside the discipline of Geography and to drive me out of academia, the more I have worked at my academic relationships and the more I have been embraced by the institutional frameworks within which I work. To borrow a rather over-used spatial metaphor, this harassment has paradoxically (re)located me both inside and outside the project.

PERSONAL GEOGRAPHIES
AND THE MEANING OF SPACE:
HOME, WORK, BODY, AND MOBILITY

Three years ago, while writing a book chapter with Lynda Johnston (Johnston and Valentine, 1995) about the performance and surveillance of lesbian identities in domestic environments, I read a lot of geographical and sociological writing about the space of "the home." In our chapter we borrowed Sommerville's (1992) seven key dimensions–shelter, hearth (emotional and physical well-being), heart (loving and caring social relations), privacy, roots (source of identity and meaningfulness), abode, and paradise ("ideal" home as distinct from everyday life)–to help us think through the complex meanings of home to the lesbians we had interviewed as part of two separate empirical studies (one in the United Kingdom, the other in New Zealand). At this time, I was in the process of buying my first house. While in our chapter we challenged the tendency within academic work on the home to privilege its positive meanings (hearth, heart, privacy, roots, paradise, and so on), pointing out the alienation and oppression experienced by some of our interviewees at home, my own sympathies at that time lay with the sentiments expressed by Peter Saunders (1989:184) when he wrote, "The home is where people are offstage, free from surveillance, in control of their immediate environment. It is their castle. It is where they feel they belong."

I fell in love with my house the day I first saw it. Spending time alone in other houses, I have occasionally felt uneasy at night. But from the day I moved into my home in Sheffield, despite initially having no carpets or furniture, I have always felt completely safe and at ease. Not only did my own home provide shelter, hearth, security, it was my first taste of absolute privacy–previously I had always lived with other people (parents, co-tenants, landladies, partners) in the space that they had largely created and that they ultimately regulated.

My first home was my first chance to create my own space through furniture, pictures, and so on. Writing about the moral economy of the household, Silverstone et al. (1992:19-20) argue:

> Objects and meanings, in their objectification and incorporation within the spaces and practices of domestic life, define a particular semantic universe for the household in relation to that offered in the public world of commodities and ephemeral and instrumental relationships. But they do so through an evaluative–a moral–project, which in turn results in the creation of a spatially and temporally bounded sense of security and trust, a sense of security and trust without which (indeed any) life would become impossible.

And so it has been for me. But not only are my pictures and my stereo appropriated into my personal economy of meaning, so too are my telephone and the letter box. As someone who has spent a lot of my adult life on the move, I have managed to accumulate clusters of friends who are spatially distributed around the country in a pattern that defies conventional measures of social network density. The telephone and the letter box have become symbols of connection–mediators of the cultural pleasures of friendship. I always start the day by checking my post, and my phone bill epitomises Bob Hoskins' advertising slogan that "it's good to talk."

It is into this meaningful space–which I considered a more or less impermeable, bounded, safe environment, of which I was in total control–that the hate mail, calls, and nighttime disturbances have intruded. The letters and calls have disrupted the taken-for-grantedness of my domestic life. Giddens (1989:287) defines "ontological security" as "a sense of confidence or trust in the world as it appears to be." But my world is no longer as it appears to be. Simple objects (the envelope), everyday sounds (the phone ringing) have taken on new meanings, meanings laden with threat, potent with menace. In *In*

Place/Out of Place, Cresswell (1996) argues that we have expectations about how we are supposed to behave in places–normative landscapes–that are often only evident when they are transgressed. He uses
several examples, including the Greenham Common Women's Peace
Camp, graffiti in New York City, and the Stonehenge Festival, to show
how individuals and groups can "question and resist the 'way things
are' by (mis)using and appropriating already existing places and by
crossing boundaries that often remain invisible" (Cresswell, 1996:
175). He goes on to demonstrate through each of his case studies how
through acts of transgression the existing landscape is brought into
question and alternative ones are hinted at. He writes, "The crossing
of established sociogeographical boundaries upsets the status quo and
appears shocking. It is perceived as grotesque, as threatening" (Cresswell, 1996:176).

I like this work–I have used notions of transgression to think about
the way lesbians and gay men can disrupt the taken-for-granted production of everyday space as heterosexual space (Bell et al., 1994;
Bell and Valentine, 1995; Valentine, 1996b). It has always seemed
such a playful concept, epitomised in my mind by visions of lesbian
avengers invading window displays in one of London's major shopping streets, posing next to mannequins with labels such as Designer
Dyke, Lesbian Boy, Funky Femme.[9] But suddenly I have lost my
sense of humour because it is my expectations about behaviour in my
place–my "normative landscape," the taken-for-granted beliefs and
practices in my home and my neighbourhood–that have been transgressed. Someone has crossed lines that are not meant to be crossed. I
no longer know quite how to recognise and react to the spatial text of
my neighbourhood. From interviewing lesbians as part of my research, I am all too well aware that homophobic harassment can include faeces through letter boxes, acid on cars, and so on. Twice in the
early hours of the morning, I have been convinced that there was
someone outside the house; once someone rang the doorbell at 4 a.m.,
and one late-night silent call was traced to a phone box located in a
street near my home. My awareness is heightened to every possible
change in my environment–to a clue that my harasser has been there.
Little signs that I would not have even noticed before my home space
was transgressed, let alone attributed with any significance, have taken
on new meanings. The scratches on my garage door–where did they
come from? Were they there before? How to read the trail of matches

up the alleyway leading to my backyard–is it a sign of my neighbour's clumsiness lighting up? Or should I read it as a threatening sign from my harasser? The car engine running outside in the early hours of the morning–a waiting taxi? Or a surveillant stalker? I can no longer distinguish what is "in place" or what is "out of place" in my own neighbourhood. While my friends have tried to reassure me that anyone who sends malicious mail must by definition be a coward who is unlikely to escalate the "violence" further, it is always in the back of my mind that the harassment might progress from hate mail to more direct forms of violence. Certainly most of the letters contain an implicit threat of physical harm:

> I think [X] and [Y] [my parents] should hear what I've heard about you[,] you nasty piece of dyke scum. You're not fit to breathe air[,] sick bitch. You will go to hell. (Letter 2)

> EVER POURED SALT ON A SLUG? STAY OUT OF THE SEA THIS SUMMER. (Letter 8)

It is not only the meaning and security of my home that are being threatened, but also the meaning of my department as a workplace. This space, too, has been invaded by the letters. Instead of an excuse to take a break, the arrival of the morning and afternoon post has become an occasion of dread. As I hinted in my discussion of academic networks and confidence in the previous section, my workplace (including the virtual workplace), like my home, has been recoded from a safe space where I felt in control into an uncertain, unpredictable, and threatening world, as Letter 9 (Figure 9) demonstrates:

> Has anyone told you about the web page? We just about have enough material now. It should be a scream. It will also show the world what you really are–a sick menace who shouldn't be allowed anywhere near kids. We'll be sending the address out soon. Don't worry, the fall from the cess pool [sic] you dwell in won't be too hard.

There are physiological aspects to this, too, that have exposed my own pollution anxieties and the extent to which my stalker is hovering at the borders of my identity, threatening the boundaries of my notion of self. Opening Letter 8 (Figure 8), I suddenly began to gag and choke. Since then, whenever I feel stress, this sensation of retching returns. The throat is a locus of the exchange between inside and outside. It is as if my body is defending itself against the filth of the letters, by expelling the poison.[10]

In these ways, the letters have violated most of the important spaces of my existence: from my body, home, parents' home, and neighbourhood to my workplace and sense of academic community. In doing so, they have highlighted to me how much my sense of security, my well-being, and my multiple subjectivities are anchored to these locations–and consequently both how much I have a personal geography and how much I had taken it for granted until it was transgressed. Now that all these spaces can be and are being invaded and violated, I have no escape from the harassment–I cannot change my home, my parents' address, and my work address in the way that I can potentially attempt to change a telephone number; I cannot secure the boundaries of these spaces. Addresses locate us or more accurately pinpoint us in space, and in doing so they can make us vulnerable. Instead of finding a sense of emotional and physical well-being, privacy, security, and so on at home, now I find peace in mobility. Weekends away and even a field class have become sanctuaries–a refuge from the locatedness and hence the vulnerability of my address. On the move, I cannot be invaded, I cannot be violated.

"Space," it would seem, is the key to understanding how and why the processes of harassment that I have experienced have been so powerful and at times effective.

My recognition of this fact also brought home to me a rather ironic paradox between the intentions of my harasser in writing the letters and the effects that they have actually produced. While my harasser has been using my identity as a lesbian (sexual self) to attempt to undermine my identity as a geographer (academic self), trying to understand these experiences of harassment has made me think about my personal geography, which in turn has solidified my belief in the importance of Geography as a spatial discipline and in my own academic identity as a geographer. In this way, Geography and my multiple subjectivities seem to be inextricably constituted by or bound up with each other.

FIGHTING BACK: GEOGRAPHIES OF THE LAW

When I received the first letter, I telephoned two friends and asked their advice about what to do. They were both adamant that I should call the police immediately. I was more hesitant.

Reviewing geographical work on the law, Chouinard (1994:426) notes that Blomley (1989) has proposed a conception of law as an interpretative process that takes place in diverse communities. She goes on to argue for the need to think about the processes involved in shaping people's positions as legal subjects and their capacities to act within and outside the legal system, challenging perspectives that treat the interpretative process within official arenas of discourse (for example, the courts) as the key locus of empowerment or disempowerment. She points out that many people do not have access to these forums in the first place and that this approach fails to recognise how the exercise and experience of legal power are embedded in complex lived relations of daily life and diverse conditions of discourse and struggle. In summarising Kobayashi's (1990) work, Chouinard (1994:427) writes that "processes of formulating, interpreting and enforcing law are, albeit not always obviously so, rooted within specific ways of life, material conditions of struggle and lived social relations which empower some groups and voices while marginalizing, oppressing and silencing others."

My experience of doing research on both women's fear and lesbian geographies has acquainted me with numerous examples of the fact that the law is constituted within prevailing relations of inequality and oppression–for example, patriarchy and heterosexism–and so incorporates assumptions and practices associated with these social relations (Smart, 1989). Describing the fact that discrimination on the basis of sexual orientation in relation to employment, housing, and other services is, with the exception of only a few states and municipalities, legal within the United States, Herek states that "[g]ay men and lesbians . . . remain largely outside the law" (1992:91). Not surprisingly, numerous surveys (Comstock, 1989; Gross et al., 1988) suggest that hate crimes are grossly underreported because lesbians and gay men think the police are homophobic and because they fear public disclosure of their sexuality if a case they are involved in should go to court. To give just one example, von Schulthess (1992) reports that of the 226 lesbians she interviewed who had been victimised because of their sexuality, only 15 had reported their experiences to the police. It is also well documented that those lesbians and gay men who do have the courage to report their experiences commonly encounter secondary victimisation at the hands of the courts and the media, who are indifferent or hostile to victims of hate crimes (Berrill and Herek, 1992).

With these studies in mind, my academic self was extremely skeptical about the reception that a complaint about homophobic harassment might receive from the South Yorkshire police and of the consequences of pursuing it; my lesbian self–who had witnessed at first hand the attitude of the police to sexual dissidents during the anti-Clause 28 demonstrations in 1988–not unreasonably was loath to even contemplate making a complaint and fearful of being "outed" to my parents through any associated court case (although, of course, subsequently my harasser removed this inhibition by outing me to my parents), while my white, middle-class, law-abiding self was adamant that it was important to do the "right thing" and that I would get justice. These multiple past experiences of the law, combined with my complex readings of the present law as an academic, a lesbian, and a white middle-class woman, have produced me as a rather contradictory legal subject in which I simultaneously occupy different subject positions in and against the legal system (MacKinnon, 1989; Chouinard, 1994).

It was after much deliberation and with some trepidation that I eventually called the police. Initially, it was a very empowering experience. My stereotypical assumption about the heterosexism of the legal system was exploded when the officer sent to see me turned out to be a lesbian herself–a case perhaps of boundaries turning out to be connections. She was both very sympathetic and very optimistic about a successful conclusion to the case.

The letters I received were sent for fingerprinting and, despite the difficulties of obtaining prints from paper, actually yielded (frustratingly, some months later) several useful impressions. These have yet to be compared with the fingerprints of the suspect. Under the Protection against Harassment Act passed in 1997, the malicious mail potentially constitutes an arrestable criminal offence punishable by a maximum prison sentence of five years and an unlimited fine.[11] The harassment is also a lesser offence under other acts, including the Communications Act (1988) and the Offences against the Person Act (1861). Silent calls are an offence under the Telecommunications Act (1984). Indeed, the Court of Appeal has held that a telephone call or series of silent calls could constitute an assault occasioning actual bodily harm where the victim experiences significant psychological symptoms–interestingly from a geographical point of view, raising the prospect of "long-distance," disembodied interpersonal violence.

While definitions of bodily harm are not necessarily predicated on bodily presence–recognising perhaps that subjectivity is not physically or materially tied to the body–the suspect's embodiment is more crucial in defining what constitutes grounds for arrest. Despite circumstantial evidence that points the finger at a geographer within my own social networks, the police need to catch a material body in the act or its traces (for example, fingerprints) before they can make an arrest.

Initially, I felt completely empowered by the response of the police to my complaint and actually wanted another letter to arrive to increase the chance of obtaining more and better-quality fingerprints. But slowly my sense of control and optimism has been dissipated as the fingerprinting process has dragged on, as the police have failed to update me on the progress of the investigation, and as the mail has become more and more malicious and invasive.[12]

The legal system invites complainants to believe that "help" or "justice" is out there, symbolised by the law; instead, my experiences have brought home to me the realisation that ultimately empowerment lies within the self. When I was writing my PhD thesis on women's fear of violence, I read a number of studies (Glass and Singer, 1972; Rachman, 1978) about the psychology of fear that argued that the root cause of fear is a perception of helplessness and a sense of lack of control (which can in turn lead to depression and ultimately death). These studies have suggested that taking some form of control or initiative, even in a very minor way, can actually break cycles of helplessness and fear. With this in mind, inspired by my current research on children's use of the World Wide Web, I recently began to use the Internet to look for information on how to deal with being harassed, an example perhaps of the global informing the local. It was also to counter my feelings of helplessness that I first embarked on writing this paper. And so in these ways, too, to paraphrase the quotation from Rose (1997:316) I used in the introduction, my geographical research and selves have become "interactive texts."

HAPPYISH ENDINGS?

In this paper I have tried to use some events from my own life to outline a geography of what it means to be harassed. In exploring the way that hate mail and silent phone calls have invaded most of the important spaces in my everyday-life world, I have come to recognise not only the significance of my personal geography to my sense of ontological security (and how much I have taken this for granted until it has been transgressed), but also the value of Geography as a discipline in helping me to understand my experiences, which in turn has reconfirmed my academic identity as a geographer.

In trying to understand how my subjectivity has been shaped by these particular experiences, I think it necessary to reflect on the Gill-then–the Gill before the harassment–and the Gill-now. The process of coming out is often spoken of as if it is a one-off choice of being in or out. Yet in reality it is a more complex, messy, and continual process. Prior to being outed to my parents and writing this paper, I existed in a messy limbo of assumption. Within the discipline of Geography, I was assumed to be an "out" lesbian, while actually being quite closeted; within my family, I was assumed to be heterosexual, while in the public world, I was an "out" lesbian (indeed, the *Gay Times* recently included David Bell and me in a list of the 100 most influential gay men and lesbians in the country!). I was the living embodiment of Bill Clinton's "don't ask, don't tell" U.S. military policy. I was able to negotiate these contradictions by keeping these different performances of my identity distanced in space and time. Yet these messy contradictions also placed me in a situation of vulnerability. The abusive harassment I have experienced, "outing" me to my parents and "inspiring" me to officially "come out" within Geography through writing this paper, has effectively exploded some of the boundaries–albeit rather unstable ones (especially when my father discovered the Internet and started looking for my home page)–that, until this point, I had so carefully maintained between home and work, the personal and the political, and the private and the public–and has therefore exploded some of the contradictions among my lesbian self, my academic self, my family self, and my research.

In doing so, the harassment has made transparent the extent to which my sexual identity as a lesbian has shaped my research and how this has shaped my academic identity. In turn, by using a list of my research publications on lesbian geographies to "out" me to my parents, my harasser has effectively used my research and academic identity to constitute my sexual identity in the eyes of my family. In this way, my sexual identity, my geographical research and writing, and my identity as an academic have been mutually constitutive of each other.

By "coming out" in this paper, I am temporarily unifying these multiple subjectivities by enacting the identity of an "out" lesbian-geographer. Yet, of course, I am no more a unified, coherent self now than I was "then" (in my limbo of complex assumptions). One of the criticisms of "coming-out stories" (for example, Penelope and Wolfe, 1980; Hall Carpenter Archives/Lesbian Oral History Group, 1989) is that they are often told as if the momentary realisation of a sexual identity suddenly makes sense of a previously incomprehensible and confused self, from which emerges a more authentic or better self (Martin, 1988; Stanley, 1992). I do not want this paper to be read in that way. I do not want the fact that I have temporarily made my identity as a lesbian-geographer more certain by enacting it in this paper to foreclose the fact that I remain–to paraphrase the Gibson-Graham (1994) quotation that I first used in the introduction–an un-centred, uncertain, complex, divided, and not fully representable sub-ject. In particular, I do not like positions of "representativity," what Miller (1991:x) terms the incantatory recital of "speaking as a" and the imperialisms of "speaking for." She writes:

> *Did being Jewish really mean I always wanted to speak "as a Jew"* and be spoken as one? *The short answer is no, I have not found a way to assume that rhetoric of identity (although I am both, I cannot lay claim to "Jewish feminist"); it is not a ground of action for me in the world, nor the guarantee of my politics–or writing. The fact, however, of being both Jewish and a feminist is a crucial, even constitutive piece of my self-consciousness as a writer; and in that sense of course it is also at work-*on occasion-*in the style and figures of my autobiographical project. . . . The narrative of these occasions is necessarily locational: it is what happens to theory in the flesh of practice, in the social spaces of institutional life.* (Miller, 1991:97, italics and Roman text as in the original)

If there is a conclusion to this paper (which to date there certainly is not to my story of harassment), I think that my experiences demon-strate that when power is exercised–in this case through silent calls and hate mail–it does not have singular or uniform effects but multi-ple (even contradictory) outcomes and it can rebound with conse-quences that were not intended. Certainly, my experiences have been deeply painful, traumatic, and destructive, and I do not want to play down the extent to which they have affected my home life, my family, my work, and my sense of health and well-being. But at the same time, some of the harm intended depended on my reading the material in the way the author intended (that I am being excluded from the discipline by a collective group of geographers) and on other people reacting to it in the way intended (for example, by my parents disowning me). Instead, by reporting the harassment to the appropriate institutions and authorities, by seeking support from colleagues and friends, and by trying to unpack my experiences through writing this paper, I have forged new connections and honesty in my relationships, have returned to working on sexuality, and have felt more embraced by the discipline of Geography. Perhaps this realisation of how the harassment has strengthened my personal and professional position more than anything else will stop my harasser from trying to victimise me.

ACKNOWLEDGMENTS

I will never be able to repay the debt of friendship, loyalty, and support shown to me by Sarah, Sarah, Ali, Joan, Deborah, and Laura during the last year. Annie, Gregor, Liz, Nigel, Cara, Jon, Andy, Trude, and Andy have also played an important part in keeping my spirits up.

I'm grateful to various members of the South Yorkshire Police and the Personnel Department of the University of Sheffield for restoring my faith in the open-mindedness, albeit not the effectiveness, of their respective institutions; and to Alistair, Ben, Pat, Lake, and Andrew for disproving my academic skepticism about the existence of neighbourhood community.

As writing this paper has caused me to reflect on my career, I would also like to take this opportunity to thank a number of geographers who at different moments have provided me with intellectual encouragement and practical support in the form of advice, job references, and so on: Dave Thomas, Sophie Bowlby, Peter Dicken, Doreen Massey, Linda McDowell, Ian Gordon, Chris Philo, Cindi Katz, Stuart Aitken, Janet Townsend, Mike Bradford, Ian Simmons, Richard Munton, Rob Ferguson, Gwyn Rowley, Peter Smithson, Harvey Armstrong, and Peter Jackson.

At several moments when my confidence was in pieces, kind words (and deeds) about my research or teaching from a number of academics and students helped to rescue me (unbeknown to them) from my despair. In particular, I'd like to thank Peter Taylor, Dave Matless, Hester Parr, Allison James, Ginny Morrow, David Buckingham, Tristan Palmer, Kim Van Eyck, Rachel Burrows, Tom-Delph Januirek, and Janet Elsden.

I am very grateful to Liz Bondi, Sarah Holloway, Ali Grant, and Ron Martin for their comments on a previous draft of this paper, although the final product and any errors contained within remain my sole responsibility. I'd also like to thank Graham Allsopp and Jody Gordon for their technical help in reproducing the figures. Finally, I wish to say a particular thank you to Linda McDowell, not only for her comments on the manuscript, but for the sensitive way in which she and the *Antipode* team at Blackwell (Anne Jones, Becky Kennison, and Martha Sullivan) handled the publication of this article.

NOTES

1. Most notably the contributors to the original Women and Geography Study Group book, *Gender and Geography* (1984).

2. Interestingly, undergraduates have not assumed that my research and sexual identity are mutually constitutive. Recently, on a field class, I was in a pub with some students, and they started talking to me about the book I coedited with David Bell on geographies of sexualities, *Mapping Desire*–a text used in their core social geography module. Then out of the blue one of the students said, "Do you mind if I ask you something really personal?" So I braced myself for what seemed to me the inevitable question, only to be asked whether I "fancied" one of the male physical geography members of the staff.

3. These are reproduced from copies of the originals on the following pages with some edits to remove personal information relating to other people. The originals have been retained by the South Yorkshire Police as evidence in their ongoing investigation of this criminal offence.

4. When it was announced that the actress Ellen DeGeneres was going to publicly come out as a lesbian on her American television show, North American lesbian and gay groups started a campaign to encourage people to "come out" with Ellen. At the time, I joked that if the episode was broadcast in the UK, I might take the plunge and come out with Ellen, too. Ironically, my harasser outed me to my parents in the very week when the Ellen coming-out episode was actually broadcast in the UK (nearly one year after its North American screening).

5. I am certain that this harassment is not linked to any of these experiences nor to individuals implicated in these incidents.

6. Apologies to other members of the Sexuality and Space Network who don't see it like this.

7. I am certain that the letters are not in any way related to these individuals.

8. During the period of this harassment, I have missed several deadlines. I am grateful to the various book and journal editors who have accepted my grovelled apologies and hope that this paper also now serves as a partial explanation for my inefficiency.

9. I am not, however, suggesting that Cresswell and others who have used the concept to such effect have meant it to be employed in the way that I am using it here.

10. I have also suffered from insomnia and bad dreams.

11. If any reader has been asked to address envelopes to me or to post letters to me from different locations–perhaps under the illusion that it was part of a practical joke–please contact me in confidence at G.Valentine@sheffield.ac.uk. I would also

be grateful for any information about anyone who, in the light of this paper, has appeared to show a disproportionate interest in my life, who has asked questions about my activities, talked excessively about me, or spread disparaging stories about my relationships, my work, or my working relationships in different departments.

12. At the time of writing, the investigation is still ongoing.

REFERENCES

Bell, D. (1991) Insignificant others: lesbian and gay geographies. *Area* 23:323-329.

Bell, D. (1994) Erotic topographies: on the Sexuality and Space Network. *Antipode* 26:96-100.

Bell, D., and G. Valentine (1995) The sexed self: strategies of performance, sites of resistance. In S. Pile and N. Thrift (Eds.) *Mapping the Subject: Geographies of Cultural Transformation.* London: Routledge, pp. 143-157.

Bell, D., J. Binnie, J. Cream, and G. Valentine (1994) All hyped up and no place to go. *Gender, Place, and Culture* 1:31-47.

Berrill, K.T., and G.M. Herek (1992) Primary and secondary victimisation in anti-gay hate crimes: official responses and public policy. In G.M. Herek and K.T. Berrill (Eds.) *Hate Crimes: Confronting Violence against Lesbians and Gay Men.* London: Sage, pp. 289-305.

Binnie, J. (1997) Coming out of geography: towards a queer epistemology. *Environment and Planning D: Society and Space* 15:223-237.

Blomley, N. (1989) Text and context: rethinking the law-space nexus. *Progress in Human Geography* 11:512-534.

Bondi, L. (1997) Stages on journeys: some remarks about human geography and psychotherapeutic practice. Paper presented at the Inaugural International Conference in Critical Geography, 9-13 August, Vancouver, British Columbia (available from the author at Department of Geography, University of Edinburgh, Edinburgh EH8 9XP, UK).

Butler, J. (1990) *Gender Trouble: Feminism and the Subversion of Identity.* London: Routledge.

Chouinard, V. (1994) Geography, law and legal struggles: which ways ahead? *Progress in Human Geography* 18:415-440.

Chouinard, V., and A. Grant (1995) On being not even anywhere near "the project": revolutionary ways of putting ourselves in the picture. *Antipode* 27:137-166.

Comstock, G.D. (1989) Victims of anti-gay/lesbian violence. *Journal of Interpersonal Violence* 4:101-106.

Cresswell, T. (1996) *In Place/Out of Place: Geography, Ideology and Transgression.* Minneapolis: University of Minnesota Press.

Gibson-Graham, J.K. (1994) Stuffed if I know!: reflections on post-modern feminist social research. *Gender, Place, and Culture* 1:205-224.

Giddens, A. (1989) A reply to my critics. in D. Held and J.B. Thompson (Eds.) *Social Theory of Modern Societies: Anthony Giddens and His Critics.* Cambridge: Cambridge University Press, pp. 249-301.

Glass, D., and J. Singer (1972) Urban Stress. London: Academic Press.

Grant, A. (1997) Dyke geographies: all over the place. In G. Griffin and S. Andermaker (Eds.) *Straight Studies Modified: Lesbian Interventions in the Academy.* London: Cassell, pp. 115-129.

Gross, L., S.K. Aurand, and R. Adessa (1988) *Violence and Discrimination against Lesbian and Gay People in Philadelphia and the Commonwealth of Pennsylvania.* Philadelphia: Philadelphia Lesbian and Gay Task Force (available from the Philadelphia Lesbian and Gay Task Force, 1501 Cherry Street, Philadelphia, PA 19102).

Hall Carpenter Archives/Lesbian Oral History Group (Eds.) (1989) Inventing Ourselves: Lesbian Life Stories. London: Routledge.

Herek, G.M. (1992) The social context of hate crimes: notes on cultural heterosexism. In G.M. Herek and K.T. Berrill (Eds.) *Hate Crimes: Confronting Violence against Lesbians and Gay Men.* London: Sage, pp. 89-104.

Johnson, L. (1994) What future for feminist geography? *Gender, Place, and Culture* 1:103-113.

Johnston, L., and G. Valentine (1995) Wherever I lay my girlfriend that's my home: the performance and surveillance of lesbian identities in domestic environments. In D. Bell and G. Valentine (Eds.) *Mapping Desire: Geographies of Sexualities.* London: Routledge, pp. 99-113.

Katz, C. (1992) All the world is staged: intellectuals and the projects of ethnography. *Environment and Planning D: Society and Space* 10:495-510.

Kobayashi, A. (1990) Racism and law in Canada: a geographical perspective. *Urban Geography* 11:447-473.

Kristeva, J. (1982) *Powers of Horror: Essays on Abjection.* New York: Columbia University Press.

MacKinnon, C. (1989) *Towards a Feminist Theory of the State.* Cambridge, MA: Harvard University Press.

Martin, B. (1988) Lesbian identity and autobiographical difference/s. In B. Brodzki and C. Schenck (Eds.) *Life/Lines: Theorising Women's Autobiography.* Ithaca, NY: Cornell University Press, pp. 77-103.

McDowell, L. (1990) Sex and power in academia. *Area* 22:4.

McDowell, L. (1992) Doing gender: feminism, feminist and research methods in human geography. *Transactions of the Institute of British Geographers* 17:399-416.

McNay, L. (1994) *Foucault: A Critical Introduction.* Cambridge: Polity Press.

Miller, N.K. (1991) *Getting Personal: Feminist Occasions and Other Autobiographical Acts.* London: Routledge.

Moss, P. (1998) A sojourn into the autobiographical: researching chronic illness. Unpublished paper (available from the author at Department of Geography, University of Victoria, Victoria, BC V8W 3P5, Canada).

Okely, J., and H. Callaway (1992) *Anthropology and Autobiography.* London: Routledge.

Penelope, J., and S. Wolfe (Eds.) (1980) *The Original Coming Out Stories.* San Francisco: Crossing Press.

Rachman, 5.1. (1978) *Fear and Courage.* Harmondsworth: Penguin.

Rose, G. (1993) *Feminism and Geography.* Cambridge: Polity.

Rose, G. (1997) Situating knowledges: positionality, reflexivities and other tactics. *Progress in Human Geography* 21:305-320.

Saunders, P. (1989) The meaning of "home" in contemporary English culture. *Housing Studies* 4:177-192.

Sibley, D. (1995) *Geographies of Exclusion.* London: Routledge.

Silverstone, R., E. Hirsch, and D. Morley (1992) Information and communication technologies and the moral economy of the household. In R. Silverstone and E. Hirsch (Eds.) *Consuming Technologies: Media and Information in Domestic Spaces.* London: Routledge, pp. 15-31.

Smart, C. (1989) *Feminism and the Power of Law.* London: Routledge.

Sommerville, P. (1992) Homelessness and the meaning of home: rooflessness or rootedness? *International Journal of Urban and Regional Research* 16:528-539.

Stanley, L. (1992) *The Auto/biographical I.* Manchester: Manchester University Press.

Valentine, G. (1989) The geography of women's fear. *Area* 21:385-390.

Valentine, G. (1993a) (Hetero)sexing space: lesbian perceptions and experiences of everyday spaces. *Environment and Planning D: Society and Space* 11:395-413.

Valentine, G. (1993b) Negotiating and managing multiple sexual identities: lesbian time-space strategies. *Transactions of the Institute of British Geographers* 18:237-248.

Valentine, G. (1993c) Desperately seeking Susan: geographies of lesbian friendships. *Area* 25:109-116.

Valentine, G. (1996a) An equal place to work?: anti-lesbian discrimination and sexual citizenship in the European Union. in M.D. Garcia-Ramon and J. Monk (Eds.) *Women of the European Union: The Politics of Work and Daily Life.* London: Routledge, pp. 111-125.

Valentine, G. (1996b) (Re)negotiating the "heterosexual street": lesbian productions of space. In N. Duncan (Ed.) *BodySpace: Destabilising Geographies of Gender and Sexuality.* London: Routledge, pp. 146-155.

von Schulthess, B. (1992) Violence in the streets: anti-lesbian assault and harassment in San Francisco. In G.M. Herek and K.T. Berrill (Eds.) *Hate Crimes: Confronting Violence against Lesbians and Gay Men.* London: Sage, pp. 65-73.

Women and Geography Study Group of the institute of British Geographers (1984) *Gender and Geography: An Introduction to Feminist Geography.* London: Hutchinson.

Women and Geography Study Group of the Institute of British Geographers (1997) *Feminist Geographies: Explorations in Diversity and Difference.* Harlow: Longman.

Road Trip Diary/Journal de Route:
An Extract from the Installation

Cyndra MacDowall

SUMMARY. The following photo/text work is an extract from a much larger installation of photographs and text. The photographs have a modified generic quality: colour landscapes and self-portraits in tourist sites across America, the images similar to postcards or amateur tourist/family photographs. The stories, by contrast, are grounded in an individual specificity of response to the sites and events of the trip to function as allegorical anecdotes. The work conjoins a personal, lesbian and poetic narrative with familiar and potentially mundane images. The format of the tourist plaque is an appropriation of the trope of 'official' authority that uses such markers to direct and define what is currently *and* historically significant.

The work explores questions of: the ambiguity of identity through association, lesbian invisibility, cross gender play, homo/lesbo eroticism, women's access to and ownership of public space, the imaginary of the 'road trip,' landscape in photography, the documentary function of photography, photographic history, heterosexual assumption, etc. The work constructs a lesbian cognitive map of space, place, memory and history. The work (initially) appears simple in presenting familiar imagery with personal stories that explore theoretical ideas of lesbian subjecthood. *[Article copies available for a fee from The Haworth Document Delivery Service: 1-800-342-9678. E-mail address: getinfo@haworthpressinc.com <Website: http:// www.haworthpressinc.com>]*

KEYWORDS. Lesbian narrative, identity, road trip, landscape, (in)visibility

---

Cyndra MacDowall, MFA, is Lecturer in Photography at the University of Toronto/Sheridan College.

Address correspondence to: Cyndra MacDowall, Art and Art History Program, Sheridan College, 1430 Trafalgar Road, Oakville, Ontario, Canada, L6H 2Ll.

All photographs originally in colour.

[Haworth co-indexing entry note]: "Road Trip Diary/Journal de Route: An Extract from the Installation." MacDowall, Cyndra. Co-published simultaneously in *Journal of Lesbian Studies* (Harrington Park Press, an imprint of The Haworth Press, Inc.) Vol. 4, No. 1, 2000, pp. 113-124; and: *From Nowhere to Everywhere: Lesbian Geographies* (ed: Gill Valentine) Harrington Park Press, an imprint of The Haworth Press, Inc., 2000, pp. 113-124. Single or multiple copies of this article are available for a fee from The Haworth Document Delivery Service [1-800-342-9678, 9:00 a.m. - 5:00 p.m. (EST). E-mail address: getinfo@haworthpressinc.com].

113

He proposed we take this road trip together
His agenda is clear–the missile grids.

My purpose is less specific. l want to see the desert.
My goal is New Mexico and Arizona.
I know that in traveling with him l will be seen as his partner.

He is my guide to America and he brings all his road myths
with him.
He expects my recognition.
I know the stories of freedom and the highway,
The pursuit of self and self-knowledge through the road.
Besides, they are all about traveling, never arriving.

We are both the same age.
Neither of us has a model for keeping alive in our forties.
All his road myths are about young men.
They never seemed to fit me.

FIGURE 1. Normalville, PA, 1995

To be constantly invisible is wearing.
Together, we fulfill the glancing expectation of the norm.
We make an agreement to go to girl bars
in any of the towns that have one.

In Hot Springs, Arkansas, we have lunch at Grandma's.
The interior decoration is all W.W. II memorabilia.
On the way out I go to the cash and pay both our bills.
While I'm waiting for change,
the waitress comes to tell me that my husband has left his
glasses behind.
I don't correct her.

He is nervous every time we enter a girl bar.
An occasional smoker, he always enters smoking.
I'm not sure what he expects, and I never ask him.
I always check with the bar in advance to make sure it's okay to
bring him.
We usually end up playing pool.
He's a social liability, here.

FIGURE 2. Mirror Me, Art Plaza, 1995

I look at our lives over the past decade.
He took many road trips like this one;
he's told me stories about them.
My journeys have been inside me–into myself,
Now I want public space.

I stand in front of this church–a landmark,
made familiar by Strand, Adams, and O'Keeffe.
I set up a shot, and ask him to take it.

I want to be unobtrusive.
Making photographs has always been an intimate process for me,
a close engagement with my subject.
It's different in public.

FIGURE 3. San Francesco de Assis Church, Taos, NM, 1995

Corn Palace, Mitchell, South Dakota
Standing in front of the Corn Palace,
while he is taking my picture from across the street, I feel eyes
on me.
I am accustomed to being sneered at in the Midwest,
but these are interested eyes–I'm being cruised.
I look around seeking the source. I find her.
Our eyes briefly connect.
We are both in motion, going in opposite directions.
She's carrying a big gray video camera and is with a woman,
my confirmation.
She sees that I'm with him and disappears into the Corn Palace.

FIGURE 4. Corn Palace, Mitchell, SD, 1995

Dike, Iowa
We've been driving in the Midwest for days now.
The land is flat and dusty, with clusters of greenery around settlements.
We pass about ten anti-abortion signs a day.
Prairies with windmills and anti-abortion billboards standing above the fields.
"Abortion Stops a Beating Heart," complete with a heart monitor line.

I'm glad that I put the rainbow sticker on the back of the car.

FIGURE 5. Water Tower, Dike, IA, 1995

FIGURE 6. Installation View of the Exhibition, Montreal, 1995

ROAD TRIP DIARY/JOURNAL DE ROUTE *INSTALLATION*

The installation is composed of two elements: 34 colour photographs, 16″ × 20″ and 34 accompanying stories, that are presented in the form of tourist plaques placed below the photographs. The original English text is translated into French and presented in both languages etched in reflective metal.

NOTES

Thanks to: Janet Rogers, Philinda Masters, Stan Denniston, Nancy Ring, Marle-Christine Simard, Paul Litherland, Penny Cousineau, The Graduate Photography Department and Concordia University, Le Conseil des Arts et des Lettres du Québec, and The Canada Council for their support and assistance with the complete exhibition and preparation of this extract. The original text is translated by Cécile Lamirande.

All photographs made with the assistance of Stan Denniston in June 1993. Exhibition 1995.

Index

AAG. *See* Association of American
    Geographers
Academic relationships, of lesbian
    researchers, 92-95,97-99,102
ACT UP, 65
Activism
    anti-violence, 7,65-68,71-76
    as cultural basis, 13,16
    regulation of, 7,63-66,71-76
    transgression as, 63-66,73,76,100
Advertisements
    employment, 62,71,73,75
    personal, 50-51,54
African Americans, perspectives of,
    15,17,54-55
African Ancestral Lesbians for
    Societal Change, 5
Age, in lesbian identity, 54
AIDS, 90
Androgynes, 52-53
Anecdotes, per tourist road trip,
    114-124
Animal names, as harassment, 86,90,
    92-93,101
Anthropology, of identity formation,
    81,87-98
Anti-abortion movement, 122
Anti-feminism
    gender hierarchy in, 65-68
    high-profile events of, 67-76
Anti-male behavior, 62,66,71,73-75
Anti-police behavior, 62,66,69-70,
    74-75
Anti-violence activism
    as feminist, 65-68
    regulation of, 71-76
Association of American Geographers
    (AAG), 86,92
Autobiographies, 81-85. *See also*
    Personal geographies

Bad girls, 42
Bars, 3,20-21,46,116
Belonging, home as place of, 12-13
Bisexuals
    discrimination of, 49,103
    in on-line space, 47-53,55-58
    term interpretation, 49,55-57
Bodily harm, protection from,
    101-102,104-105
Bookstores, alternative, 3
Boundaries
    for identity formation, 14,87-98
    setting of, 14-15,18,22,103
    transgressions of, 63-66,73,76,
    100-102,106
Brighton (England), 4
Buffer zones of sameness, 31
Butch, 53

Centrality of spatiality, 8
Clinton, Bill, 106
Co-operative living, 3,19-21
Co-operative stores, 3
Co-workers, visibility with, 18,86,
    94-95,97-98,106-108
Coming-out
    within geography research, 83-85,
    92-93,106-107
    in the home, 20-21
    as process, 106-108
    risks of, 4,65,93
    through legal system, 104-105
    in Vancouver communities, 37-38,
    38t
    in workplace, 4
Commercial Drive (Vancouver),
    34-36,34f,38-39
Communications Act (1988), 104
Community
    ambiguity of, 32-33